50 Years of Peril

One Day of Illumination That Made the Difference

Byron S. Brown

authorHOUSE®

AuthorHouse™
1663 Liberty Drive
Bloomington, IN 47403
www.authorhouse.com
Phone: 1 (800) 839-8640

Published by AuthorHouse 08/07/2017

ISBN: 978-1-5246-9961-1 (sc)
ISBN: 978-1-5246-9960-4 (e)

Print information available on the last page.

Any people depicted in stock imagery provided by Thinkstock are models, and such images are being used for illustrative purposes only. Certain stock imagery © Thinkstock.

This book is printed on acid-free paper.

Dedication

I wish to dedicate this book in loving memories of my father, Samuel George Brown and my mother, Annie Lee Charlotte Jackson Brown, for their labor of love and determination in planting a fertile seed for me to succeed in a world of great opposition and challenges.

Contents

"Every man must bear his own burden. We are constantly being challenged in order to move to the next level in life. There is no such thing as a "battle-free," life. We all grow from challenges. Through adversities, we get to know our own strengths and weaknesses. We have the power within to withstand."

Byron S. Brown

Foreword

In this life, we are often faced with the myriad factors of the unknown and the unknowable. Byron Brown has written an excellent semi-autobiographical message that resonates with the reader. His excellent details in explaining his story, his journey, his troubles and his ultimately successful outcome all within the backdrop of a memoir of respect and admiration for his Father is yet another masterpiece accomplished by the author. Mr. Brown laments in the story the loss of his father in a tragic accident. Although no fault of the senior Mr. Brown, the tragic event led to many perils and "what-ifs" for the son. Yet still, in **Fifty Years of Peril: One Day of Illumination that Made the Difference**, Byron Brown writes fearlessly in telling his story. This project was designed to coincide with the 50th anniversary of the death of Mr. Samuel George Brown, Byron's Father. It is indeed an honor and a tribute to the man that Byron missed while growing up. The spirit of his father definitely remains present by virtue of the educational, professional and familial accomplishments of Byron Brown. Further, the foundation which was set from both of his parents led to his successful life in all of these areas. For the reader of this story, you are in for a treat. The journey of life is seldom a straight river. The ebbs and flows and tides of life can often bring one to doubt or to lose faith. Yet as you will see, Byron Brown was able to overcome many adversities and doubters and with an unshakable faith bravely continued onward and upward. The inspiration garnered from this story is many faceted. When we lose loved ones, the pain never really goes away. However, if we stay the course as Byron Brown has done, then certainly the rainbows are multiplied on the other side of the scenario. As the Bible says, "His son is just like him", as this story says, although I have missed you and wondered what life would be like had you lived, perhaps you have been and are still with me on this journey after all. Finally, the continual ethos of life as a journey resonates throughout the book. With faith all things are possible; with love, remembrance and admiration of those whom we lost, the force from beyond will continue to push us through.

Stephen J. LaBrie, MBA

Introduction:

Ahalf century has come and gone since my father was killed in an automobile accident due to a person driving under the influence of alcohol. Actually, my father was the victim not the driver. For 50 years, I had to wrestle and contend with the questions, "What would life had been like for me, if my dad was not a victim in a DUI accident?" With his presence in my life, would I have had to deal with all the peril that I had to face over the past five decades? To what extent would my life have been less cumbersome? To what extent would my life have been a more improved one? How has his death impacted me as a boy, a man, a husband, a father? These are some of the perplexing questions that will never be answered throughout eternity. This tremendous sense of loss is cremated with the fire and smoke of the unknown.

It is a painful reality to know that I never had the opportunity to build a relationship with my father because his life was taken away from me when I was only two years old. One of the many realities that does come from his death is that I do love my two children, Daniel and Hannah, and I have pledged to be the best father possible to them. I so greatly want to give them what my father was never able to give me beyond my second birthday: love, joy, peace, happiness, encouragement and sound advice. All these wonderful elements would have added much happier days in my life for the past half of a century had my father lived and led me down life's highway. I certainly feel that the many bumps in the road would have been traveled much smoother had dad been present in my life. In fact, some of the thousands of bumps in the road over the past fifty years of my life never would have existed had my father lived a full life. I believe strongly that his guidance would have shed illuminating light that would have shone in paths that I would have clearly seen the dangers I had faced from 1967 to 2017. These fifty years without him and without his guidance and protection have caused me to struggle in many ways. By the grace of God, one day, I was enlightened. By being enlightened, I was afforded opportunities to forge ahead through many heavy and darks days, thus becoming a person of amazing strength, bold courage, and enduring optimism.

Fifty years of hell would not have been the appropriate title for this book because in those fifty years from September 23, 1967 to 2017, I have experienced some glorious moments. Rather, **Fifty Years of Peril** is more befitting because life was made a bit more complexed due to not having a father when I really needed him. The one day of illumination is exactly right. One smooth day in the course of my transforming life, I made a drastic decision to travel down a path that would head to many surprising and positive discoveries. As an aftermath, I became an enlightened man, thus, becoming a successful person after taking life's lemons and making lemonade.

Fifty Years of Peril: One Day of Illumination That Made the Difference in a nutshell, is a collection of stories sharing episodes of my life being lived in the danger zone, the hopeless zone, the miraculous zone, and the zone of enlightenment. Living the past fifty years without my father has indeed had its set of challenges. Living since that one day of illumination has paid off well for me. The memories of September

23, 1967, when my father became a victim of someone driving under the influence of alcohol have driven me to the point to speak out ever so strongly against drinking and driving. If the alcohol by the driver had not been consumed, my father perhaps would have lived to see his son become a man, a father, a husband, and a son of valor, respect and integrity.

Chapter 1

The Night Dad was Killed

My father stood tall, thin and dark-skinned. Many saw him as a handsome gentleman. Many remember him from loving to tell jokes. He did not let life get the best of him. Rather, he spoke with both arrogance and confidence. A few remember him using his favorite phrase to answer many questions concerning life. When he was asked how everything was, his often and immediate response, I am told, was always: "Everything's copacetic." He was a cheerful type of dude who enjoyed life. He squeezed enjoyment out of every second. He made people laughed whether they were sitting on the porch, walking down the dirt road, sitting under a tree or congregating at work. To be around him meant you wanted to have fun and be part of a circle of people who enjoyed the old oral tradition of telling and exchanging stories for laughter.

His name was Samuel George Brown and with a name as eloquent as that, he demanded respect. To those who were close to him, they could get away by calling him, Bubble. Dad loved the simple life. He loved the rural area of Eutawville, South Carolina. He had left the area with Mom to move to New York, where my oldest sister Theresa, my second oldest sister Georgetta and my oldest brother Samuel were

1

born. Because of his great love for country living, they relocated back to South Carolina. A few years later, his boss was moving his business to California and he offered Dad the opportunity to move out to California to work with him. Dad declined the offer and remained in his hometown of Eutawville, keeping his home and family intact.

Dad loved my mother. Although Mom already had enough names, Dad had to give her a name he created. So in his eyes, she was no longer called "Annie Lee," the birth name she was given. She was no longer called "Charlotte," the nick name she was given after her grandmother because Mom was a split image of her. But Dad had to give her the name: "Chabby." Chabby worked for him because he thought of it himself.

Dad was so proud of his parents. My grandparents were adorable and respectable people in the community. His mother was a Sunday School teacher and his father was a deacon at Springhill Missionary Baptist Church. Dad made it a habit to address his parents by their full name: "I am Jannie Lee Brown's son." For those who knew my grandmother, they would be so proud of Dad as he called her out by her full name. The same respect was given to my grandfather by Dad. "I am Mr. George Brown's son."

Dad was the proud brother to Mary Simmons—not just Mary. He was the proud brother to Lizzie Mae Smith—not just Lizzie Mae. The pattern continued. He was brother to Richard Brown—not just Richard. He was the brother to Nellie Barnett—not merely Nellie and finally he was the proud brother to Jannie Ruth Brown—not just Ruth. His spirit of pride for the family kept the family close together—even 50 years after his demise.

Born November 25, 1932, Dad had nothing but a bright future to look forward to each day. A promising life was instantly cut short on September 23, 1967. Dad's life spans from November 25, 1932 to September 23, 1967—a life cut off extremely too short by an individual driving under the influence of alcohol. We ought to therefore commemorate his death and send out a strong message against drinking and driving.

Dear Dad:

The past fifty years without you have presented some challenges that led up to some perilous times for me. Through your death, I have been able to develop uncommon courage. I understand that your favorite statement was "everything's copasetic." That a positive attitude you had while you lived on the earth. That is one strength I received from you. I always strive to have an optimistic viewpoint on life. Over the years, I grew to appreciate challenges, knowing that they come as stepping stones to success. Thank you for loving Mom and marrying her. She was strong and raised all of us to work hard and to love one another. Mom stepped in the gap when you were called into eternal rest. She did her very best to raise all of your children.

Thank you Dad for passing on to me your sense of humor. Many people told me that you had a wonderful sense of humor. I try to emulate you in this sense because I believe laughter is a healing tool to all misery and pain. Many times in life, I had to laugh to stop from crying. Yet, through my tears from all the perils I experienced through the fifty years you departed this life, I must admit that a sense of humor has served as a positive strategy for me to cope with the pressure in society.

Thank you for the hard-working man, husband and father you were on Earth. These are all noble deeds. I always do my very best to follow in your footsteps. Fifty years from your departure, I stand ready to rise to the occasion that I will be able to walk in your shoes with the strength, determination and optimism you used to survive on Earth.

I am proud to be your son and I hope to pass on to my son Daniel and my daughter Hannah the gift you left me—the faith to believe.

Sincerely,
Byron Brown

Chapter 2

The Fire that Almost Took My Life

I believe I was spared on this Earth for a special purpose. Not exactly sure of all the plans the Master has in place for me, I am willing to commit to serving others. I could have easily perish in my mother's house the day that the house caught on fire back in 1970. I remain grateful to yet be alive and not have perished in the fire that consumed the house that we were living in during the early 1970's. God spared the family from a major tragedy. I was not the only one in our house when it caught on fire. My brother Ricky and my two sisters Carolina and Willie Mae were in the house sitting near the wooden heater trying to stay warm while Mom was next door working in the fish market.

I believe strongly that God spared my life so that I may help spare someone else's life.

Dear Heavenly Father,

I wish to express my gratitude for your awesome power to save me from a burning fire. I cannot image the complication this would have caused the family knowing that just three to four years earlier my father was killed in an automobile accident and my baby brother David had died in a crib death. The 1960s was a difficult decade for my mother who lost her father, Boston Jackson, Sr., in the earlier part of that decade and lost her three month old son in 1966 and lost her husband in 1967. Therefore, for Mom to have lost four children in a house fire the beginning of the decade of the 1970 would have been quite devastating and unbearable to the family. Thank you ever so much for remaining faithful to your own word that you would not put more upon us than that which we can bear. A tragedy like that would have been truly unbearable.

I believe strongly that there is a purpose for keeping me on earth. I pledge to continue to seek you all the days of my life. I will strive to do as you have asked me to acknowledge you in everything I do. I cling on to this promise because you have encouraged everyone in your word that if we acknowledge you in all that we do and say, you will direct our paths.

As I close this prayer, I wish to thank you for giving our mother that extra energy and wisdom for responding in a miraculous way to save my three siblings and me from being consumed in death by the fire that destroyed our home.

Sincerely,
Byron S. Brown

Chapter 3

Sweat from the Cotton Fields

I was a member of one of the last generations to pick cotton. I remember the burning hot and sweltering days in Eutawville, South Carolina. I remember being drenched in sweat from picking cotton for only a dollar per one hundred pounds. This was during the late 1960's and early 1970s. That did not seem like much. However, when you take that one dollar and multiply it by seven or eight times, it added up. My siblings and I would pick eight to nine hundred, and on some days up to a thousand pounds of cotton. We would bring into the household $8 to $10 dollars. Back in the early seventies that was a lot of money for a family living in poverty. We enjoyed the sweat of our labor, as we were able to purchase some groceries to eat, rather than just eating our daily special of grits and poke n' beans without any meat. So picking cotton was worth it for the family as were able to eat an upgraded meal with the family.

We picked cotton for Ms. Sarah Sumpter who served as the midwife to my mother when I was ushered into the world on April 23, 1965.

It was the cotton picking days that taught me the value of working. I learned faithfully how to work as a team-player because my sibling and I had to share the rows of cotton being picked and to place them in the sack together. Ms. Sumpter was an old lady, dark-skinned and wore glasses. She was very strict. She did not like children playing around when it was time to work.

One day Ms. Sumpter made a comment that I cannot remember but I remember clearly that I did not like it. I used a swear word towards her to express my disgust with her. My mother overheard me using the swear word to Ms. Sumpter. Mom informed me that it was not nice and that I had to go to her house to apologize and I had to carry Ms. Sumpter a gift in order for her to accept my apology. So, I made up with her by carrying a can of white pet milk to her. Ms. Sumpter was so gracious of my apology and the kind deed of bringing her a can of milk that she forgave me immediately.

Picking cotton was hard work for a child under the age of ten. It seemed however that I was being taught to persevere. We would rise early in the morning, take a 30-45 minutes break from picking cotton, and we would work until late in the evening. We were developing skills that would carry us into many future years.

Dear Ms. Sarah Sumpter:

First, let me take a second to express my gratitude to you for serving as a successful mid-wife to my mother to help usher Willie Mae and me into this beautiful world. We had fun as we picked cotton in your field. It helped us out in so many ways as we suffered in poverty. The few dollars that we collectively earned weekly while picking cotton for you helped put food and drink on the table for us to consume. Although we worked in the hot heat and sweated so heavily, we did not mind. We all understood that we had to do what we had to do in order to survive. We appreciate the many benefits that working for you afforded us. The job in itself was not necessarily an easy task. We hung in the cotton fields together. It taught the family value and teamwork and appreciation for life. We grew together as a family in spite of our economic travesty. We held in there together by the grace of God as we picked cotton without complaints.

You gave us the opportunity to learn and grow as family through the vehicle of putting together one bundle of cotton after another bundle of cotton together and one day after another day in the golden ages of the cotton days. We will never forget how you helped us survive as a family. You were led by a power greater than the kind of love man can ever express inwardly or outwardly any given day.

We smile upon your grave as a person who had helped others to overcome their financial adversities in troubling times. In the simplest form of man kindness, all we can say is "Thank you."

Sincerely,
Byron Brown

Chapter 4

When the Children Laughed without Regrets

O ne of the greatest possible human disgraces is when an adult undermines and further handicaps an innocent child, especially when this happens in the field of education. Educating children is supposed to be fun, exciting, and engaging. Educators owe a great deal of commitment and loyalty to the younger generation. Educators have one profound advantage over any other careers and that is the sacred opportunity to shape minds. With this type of great influence, educators must always be mindful that they are constantly being listened to, watched and emulated. That can be a great matter of fact. However, it could simultaneously be one of the most devastating episodes if that special power is not used correctly. On both ends of the pendulum the power that an educator holds can be used to build a person or destroy a person. It all matters how a teacher uses his or her power to persuade. Teachers can engage students in how to do the right thing or they can sadly disengage a student by focusing on issues that don't matter one way or the other.

Educators should be committed to serving and helping children overcome the adversities in their individual lives. Teachers should not make the lives of students more problematic than they already are in their current state.

I feel that I have been the victim of some cruel behavior by one of my former teachers in high school. I was fortunate, however, in a way because I had a hero living in my neighborhood who stood up to that teacher because he knew that I had the potential to succeed in life. Mr. William James, Jr. listened to my claims against my teacher, whom I always refer to as Mrs. Fields, not her real name. In heroic actions, Mr. James stood in the gap for my education.

Mrs. Fields had issued what seemed to have been some very harsh words to me as a child. Her words could be misconstrued as being so bitter, so divisive, so unprofessional to utter to a child. I was defenseless as a 14 year old boy, up against a teacher who is supposed to be mature. I would have been a lost soul had I succumbed to the apparent negatively of Mrs. Fields' condescending remarks. If I had only given ears to listen to Mrs. Fields' apparently harsh words, I would not have forged ahead to make a better life for myself. It was only by the grace of God that I had my sister Willie Mae, my mother Charlotte and my next door neighbor William James, Jr. pushing me to go back to school after I had dropped out of school. Back then, I felt justified in dropping out of high school because I believed I was publicly condemned and criticized by Mrs. Fields' seemingly insensitive and untruthful words that could have led me to believe that I was stupid and could not learn.

I clearly recollect that day in high school when it seemed as though Mrs. Fields was frustrated with me because I did not understand the material she was covering and I asked her several questions to try to understand the lesson that she was covering all so quickly. I thought that I was demonstrating interest in learning by posing my questions. I felt that Mrs. Fields' sharp words came out in a tone that suggested otherwise. I had only wished it was a dream when I thought I heard her say: "You are simple. You can't learn. Are you stupid?" I wish it was only my imagination when it seemed that the entire class burst out laughing. With this thought, I held my head down in shame and disgust.

After that day, I stopped going to school. I dropped out of high school because I felt that if I was stupid and could not learn, I rationalized; what was the purpose of even going to school? This immature way of handling the situation was all my decision. I could not argue or debate with a teacher who in her own mind was far smarter than I was at the time.

The children all laughed at me when I felt Mrs. Fields mistreated me. It was painful to hear the children laughing. As I felt being bullied by her words, she had no idea that her action was building permanent scars into my life.

Dear Mrs. Fields,

I know that you have heard of my success stories one after another. It appeared that you did not believe in me. My interpretation of your action was that I was incapable of learning when I was in your class in high school. I know that my success stories speak for themselves. What seemed to have been abusive words to me caused me to temporarily drop out of high school. It was painful and embarrassing to hear all the children laughing at me, my potential, and my future as it seemed like you outrageously expressed your personal opinion of me, while I was a student in your class.

I want you to know that I forgive you for what appeared to be a lack of professional judgement in the way you seemingly appeared to make the children laugh at me as I was struggling to do the work that you gave the class.

I feel strongly that the way you treated me as a student was absolutely wrong. You must know by now that children don't forget. I was a child when I was in your class. Now I am an adult teaching my own set of students. I learned from my experiences in your class and I hope never to suppress the learning opportunities of young minds. Children are our future. We need them. We must protect them and serve them while they are in their innocent years. With hope and optimism, they in return, would protect and serve us in our golden years. That is the way it should work through the natural laws of reciprocity.

I forgive you for what appears to be a lack of understanding and may you discover room in your heart to repent and always remember that children need a clear pathway to success, in high school, college and beyond.

Sincerely,
Byron S. Brown

Chapter 5

Mugged by a Thug

Peril reign one night as I was brutally and viciously attacked. The last thing on my mind that night was the thought of being mugged by a life-long neighborhood member. It was about 12:00 midnight when my pastor, Raymond Gathers, dropped me off on the side of the road for me to walk home after a wonderful night of Christian fellowship at Cainhoy Miracle Revival Center, where mother Helen Smith led, in Huger, South Carolina. As a seventeen year old child, I had devoted my life to a Christian walk that brought much peace and joy to me as I faced so much peril during my early years of living.

Night after night, Pastor Gathers would give me a ride home after blissful church services. We attended the type of church where we clapped our hands, stomped our feet, ran around in circles and jumped for joy, all in the efforts of praising God. Services to our God included: personal testimonies, prophetic provocation and exercises of angelic laughter of joy. Our services entailed healing, deliverance and miracles. We were a special people who loved God. We were children who cried when cars were filled and there was no room for us to ride to church. In the many years of this type of routine, pastor Gathers often felt comfortable letting me out of the van on the side of the road for me to walk home. However, this night was different as he dropped me off.

Earlier that day I was very excited about the amount of money I had already saved for college. Without being aware of my inevitable attack I was counting my money in the living room as neighborhood guests came back and forth into the house visiting my sisters and brothers to play a few card games of spades. As I continued counting my money, I noticed through the corner of my eyes a prolonged watch by one of the guests—Jerry Black—when I looked up, Jerry looked at me without saying a word. He then proceeded to the kitchen where everyone was playing spades. The image of Jerry Black staring at me as I counted the money stayed with me throughout the early morning, noonday and sunset early evening. For some reason I could not shake the image out of my head.

When I had finished counting the green dollars, the silver quarters, the gray dimes, the gold nickels and the black pennies, I had counted a total of exactly one hundred dollars. I was very proud of having saved my first one hundred dollars for college. This was a huge amount for a kid to have saved in the early 1980s. It was rare enough for a kid alone to have save that amount of money faithfully as I had done. Even in the midst of peril, I desired something bigger and better for my future. I felt strongly that my life was on the correct path as I sacrificed my time for church and my money for college. I was a thoughtful and reflective kid in my hope of escaping a life of poverty and misery. I was halfway there by saving funds for college and saving my soul from sin, as I engaged in Christian fellowship with others who loved their God. Proud of saving my first one hundred dollars for college, I placed the money in a secret location by burying it in a straw basket hidden in the closet in the guest bedroom in Mom's house.

I joined the crowd in the kitchen where everyone was taking turns playing spades. As I observed them laughing and throwing one card down on the table after another with so much vigor, I also noticed that Jerry Black had disengaged himself from the fun of the game, glaring at me from head to toe. After a few minutes of feeling uncomfortable with Jerry Black watching me, I removed myself from the crowd, without acknowledging my arrival or departure.

As I disappeared into the rest of the day, I did what 17 years old boys in my neighborhood did not do. I went to my bedroom, began to read my bible, a history book and a literature book, as I practiced reading and completing grammar exercises from a grammar book. As a curious 17 year old boy, I wanted to be prepared for the tough world I was to embark upon in a year. My patience for academics grew as I was growing into a mature lad. I fell asleep in my bed with several books opened—one in my lap, one to my right side, one to my head and yet another near my feet as the rest of the day raced into early evening. Without an alarm clock, I was awaken by some thunderstorms. I had jumped out of bed realizing that it was almost time to meet Pastor Gathers for a ride to church. I had to get there as quickly as possible. I did not want to miss my ride to Cainhoy. I wanted to be in church. I wanted to see Mother Smith again, for I had grown to appreciate her as a woman of God. In fact, I was so amazed by Mother Smith's courage to answer the call she believed that she heard from God. That call was to preach the gospel to all mankind. What drew me particularly close to Mother Smith was her confession. Her confession that God had called her to preach was controversial news at the time. Mother Smith had written a book entitled: "If God Didn't Call a Woman to Preach, then Who Called Me?" That book was filled with exciting revelation that always kept my interest and put Mother Smith at a special place in my heart. It was always great learning about her sacred walk with God. Therefore, I hurried to Buddy's store to wait for Pastor Gathers to pick me up for church.

As I stepped into the gold church van we called Cindy, I felt a spirit of peace and calmness. That hour and ten minutes ride to Cainhoy Miracle Revival Center was a pleasant and soothing drive that night.

At some point during the church service, I was pulled out of my seat and drawn to the front of the church by one of the ministry's prophetess. She began to tell me what God wanted me to know about my future. She prophesied the following words to me: "My son, live holy, for danger is ahead. Danger is soon to come. Because I love you, my son, know that I will shield you. I will protect you." As she finished sharing what the Lord had to say to me, I returned to my seat rejoicing and knowing that God had promised to protect and shield me whenever I encounter or face danger.

I don't recall any more details from the service that night because I had stayed focused on the prophetic message spoken to me.

After service, Pastor Gathers had gathered all of us who had come on the van together to go back to Eutawville. When we got back to Monck Corner, he stopped at a gas station. I had two dollars on me. I went into the store and bought a can of Pepsi, a honey bun and a pack of lays potato chips. I ate this late night snack with so much grace.

When we arrived back in Eutawville, the words of the Lord again came to me from the prophecy: "I will shield you. I will protect you."

Pastor Gathers pulled up to my stop and let me out on the dirt road for me to walk home. As I got off the van saying goodnight, Evangelist Jannie Mae Graham, Sister Betty Gathers and Pastor Gathers all said: "Praise the Lord, Brother Byron."

I remained brave and unafraid as suddenly my body was being assaulted as soon as Pastor Gathers drove away. The thug who was mugging me was much larger, much taller, much older and much stronger than I was. As I was suddenly being mugged by a thug, I did not fight back. The peril of this mugging left me speechless as I took several blows from the attacker. As the thug continued to attack me, I could feel his gigantic hand reaching into my front pocket fishing for money. I felt the jerk when he forced his huge hand out of my front pockets as he moved to my back pockets searching for money. He went back and forth vigorously searching my pockets. As he came up emptied handed each time, his frustration grew, thereby causing the attacker to become more aggressive and forceful upon my body. The attacker became angrier and angrier. When he reached my last pocket and discovered I did not have any money on me, he punched me directly in the face four merciless times with each blow being thrown with all his might and strength. I was yelling and screaming, "Help, help, help." But to no avail, no one heard my desperate cry and no one came to my rescue. The attacker's forceful blows were so powerful that he knocked four of my permanent front teeth out of my mouth.

On one of my cries for help, my closet neighbor turned on a light in one of the rooms in his house. With the light being on, the thug threw my body to the ground, kicked me in my private area, and ran. As the suspect fled the scene, I became consciously aware of who he might be. I immediately surmised that he was Jerry Black. The image of Jerry Black flashed through my head as I reflected back to the early morning activities. I recalled Jerry Black looking at me strangely earlier that morning as I was counting my money to attend college. I felt 100% certain that Jerry Black was my attacker. He searched each of my pockets seeking the money I had exposed earlier that day.

As I entered the house, I awaken everybody. Mom was very upset about me being mugged. My sister Carolina had a gut feeling too that it was Jerry Black who mugged me. We all knew exactly where Jerry Black lived. My sisters Georgetta, Willia Mae and Carolina gathered at the scene of the mugging. We played detectives by following the footsteps of the attacker up to his door steps.

As we reached the attacker's house being led there successfully by his footprints in the sand, we approached his mother. We reported to her that Jerry Black had mugged me and that the shirt he was currently wearing bore my blood. The mother questioned Jerry Black in inquiring whether he attacked me or not and how did the blood get on his shirt. He flatly and immediately denied the claim. He explained that that was chicken blood. We were getting nowhere with his story. We departed with kind words. However, before we departed, we were going to call the police.

A police officer came to our house. He asked questioned and recorded information on a small spiral notebook. He then informed us that he was headed to Jerry Black's house to obtain a statement from him and then he would be back. The officer was able to verify that he observed blood on the shirt Jerry Black was wearing. He issued a citation of some sort for Jerry Black to report to court with Judge McArthur Wright.

On the date of the court session, Jerry Black could not look me directly into my eyes. If he really knew me, he would have known that I forgave him the very night he attacked me. This was true because I grew up believing that revenge was God's job and not Byron Brown's.

The Court:

Although Jerry Black had been ordered to appear in court for the damages he caused on my body, he never gave any attention to the financial obligation bestowed upon him. He never admitted his guilt. He never apologized for the permanent damages he did to my body. He never expressed regret for inflicting the emotional turmoil upon my life. He never asked me for forgiveness of his bullying attacks against my life. Growing up as a Christian, I was taught to forgive others. I was taught that if I wanted God to forgive me, I had to forgive others. Also, I was taught that if I did not forgive others, God would not forgive me because God requires us to forgive our brethren seventy times seven a day. Therefore, without restraints I immediately forgave Jerry Black for trespassing against me. In all this, I knew that God would take care of Jerry Black and that revenge was not mine but the Lord's. I knew that one day in the future Jerry Black would pay for his evil deeds. It was only a matter of time, however.

The School:

As a teenager, I had to deal with brutal harassment of the students in my senior high school class at Holly Hill-Roberts High School. When I reported back to school for the first time after I was mugged, I was expecting sympathy for being attacked by a thug. Rather, I was greeted with laughter and being teased by one student after another student. I was being harassed by them one day after another day. This type of peril lasted for the remainder of the school year. It was humiliating to be teased by the children because I had lost my four front teeth. I often concealed from smiling because if I did, everyone would have noticed it and begin picking on me and embarrassing me time and time again for not having any teeth in my mouth. Rather than succumbing to the folly of their ignorance, I chose to travel the high road opposed to the low road of life. It was not enjoyable reporting to school day after day, weeks after weeks and months after months with the pattern of being taunted endlessly. Yet, I yielded to a spirit of perseverance because I knew very well that I needed a high school diploma in order to pursue a college education.

I endured the test of time in high school, escaping the bullish attitude of the other kids who ignorantly employed harassing pressure upon my life daily by graduating June 3, 1983. It was a great feeling to shake the hands of my principal Dr. David Longshore, Jr., as he issued an 'I am proud of you Byron' smile. I was unashamed to smile back with my four missing front teeth. I did not care who saw it as I walked across the stage. This was my day and I was not going to allow anyone to spoil it. Indeed, this was the proudest day of my life.

The First Semester in College

Now that I have advanced beyond my high school days that ended on a bitter-sweet note to the multiple bullying and harassing remarks that came from some of my immature high school classmates, I felt more optimistic than ever in being a successful college student. I did not allow my high school classmates to get the best of me. I pressed toward a more promising future by putting the past behind me and entering into Morris College with renewed hope and faith to excel.

During the freshman class orientation at Morris College, we were introduced to a number of key leaders. Each stood up, introduced themselves and offered their assistance if we ever needed their advice. When the Dean of Students, Eliza Black stood up and began to speak to the class, her voice was encouraging as she invited us to consider running for class office and the Student Government Association.

My roommate and I decided that we wanted to run for office. The small conflict that arose was that he and I both wanted to be class president. We both were popular within our one week stay on campus. He was a great speaker; I was a pretty good writer. He was filled with enthusiasm and motivation with a mouth full of braces. I was warm, encouraging, and humorous with four missing teeth out of the front of my month. As roommates, he and I did not want to run against each other. We compromised. For a slight moment, I allowed my missing teeth to become an issue. I felt that my roommate would probably win the presidency since he had teeth in his mouth and I did not. So, I gave in. I encouraged him to run for president of the freshman class and I decided to run for vice president for the 1983 freshman class at Morris College. When our names were printed on the ballot, some of my classmates expressed disappointment in my decision to run for vice president. One young female said to me: "Byron, we wanted you to be our president." On election-day, my roommate was victorious winning by a margin of only seven votes over his opponent for president. I, on the other hand, received all of the 130 votes cast for vice president except for 12 over my defeated opponent. Receiving this type of victory encouraged me to strive ahead and I never looked back at the fact that I had four missing teeth in my mouth from being mugged by Jerry Black, when I was a high schooler.

My roommate rose to the stage to give his victory speech and received sporadic applauses a few times during his speech. When my name was called to give my victory speech, the audience overwhelmingly responded in a different way. When I rose to deliver my speech, the audience rose with me. When I smiled the audience smiled. When I said thank you, the audience shouted "thank you!"

"I stand today speaking before you without my four front teeth not because of a tooth decay (laughter). I am a victim of being mugged and attached one night in an attempted robbery from a suspect early that day who observed me counting my first one hundred dollars I saved to come to Morris College." The audience applauded and gave yet another standing ovation. I went on with the speech being interrupted several times with thunderous applauses and a close out ovation that lasted quite a while. This was the day of illumination for me. Their responses sparked a fire within me that never went dim.

I went on to run for president of the sophomore class and won. What were to be my third year, I ran and won the position as First Vice President of the Student Government Association. However, deeply inspired by the success at Morris College, I sought a greater challenge and thus transferred to Norfolk State University in Norfolk, Virginia in hope of exploring greater scholarship. I was determined that the attacks by Jerry Black would not deter me from becoming a success story in the coming years.

My Speech teacher at Morris College was a white nun. She was sweet and kind and lovely. Her name was Sister Donovan. One day Sister Donovan requested me to stay and see her after class. That was no problem for me since I was a patient young man and had no way to go anyhow. While in class, I was wondering the entire time, why she wanted to see me. My grades were good in her class. I had earned all A's on each of the assignment I completed. "What possibly could be the reason Sister Donovan wants to see me?" I thought to myself repeatedly. That day in class we were all doing impromptu speeches on a variety of topics. When it was my turn, I responded in such a profound way that all my college friends were amazed and there too I received many applauses. At this point, I began to realize that I had a gift for public speaking and people actually wanted to hear what I had to say. Therefore, I began to mix my gift for speaking with my talent for writing and my sense of humor to share stories of my brutal pass and no one knew I was speaking of my rough experiences growing up in Eutawville. I was good at disguising my pain, hurt and humiliation with a sense of humor. My sense of humor was one of the inherited gifts I received from my father. I have always been told that my father went from house to house making everyone in the community happy. He had a knack for making people LOL without a cellphone. I am blessed to share that gift with him.

Class had drawn to an end. I was hoping that whatever Sister Donovan had to say that it would be quick because her class was the course I was taking just before lunch. I was already hungry. I had already burned calories delivering an impromptu speech. I had already internally exhausted my brain trying to figure out why in the world did Sister Donovan want to see me that day. Lunch was the only thing left on my brain at this point.

"Byron, congratulations on your victory as being nominated vice president of the freshman class. I heard you said in your victory speech last night that you were mugged and that is how you lost the teeth in the front of your mouth."

The embarrassed and polite me, responded: "Yes, Ma'am." "It was a dude name Jerry Black. He mugged me thinking that I had a hundred dollars on me because he saw me counting my money I was saving for college. But I didn't have any money on me when he attacked me," I attempted to explain to the pleasant and curious Nun.

"Is that what happened?" the concerned Nun asked. "Oh, I am sorry Byron."

Being very particular that she did not hurt my feelings, Sister Donovan went in a long roundabout way to avoid coming across offensively to me. In a quiet and whispering tone, she asked me: "Would it be okay for me to take you to Sexton Dental Clinic in Florence, South Carolina and pay for you to get a set of denture?" Without hesitation, I immediately accepted her offer with a resounding, "yes!" My refreshed smile continued to grow wider by the seconds. That's how happy I was. My renewed smile continued growing wider as I realized for the first time in almost a half a year that I would have teeth in the front of my mouth.

I could easily discern that Sister Donovan wanted to help me so badly. She was so pleased that I accepted her generosity. Her smile was as bright and cheerful as mine. Hers was completely gay and blissful.

By the time our conversation had ended, lunch too had ended. With this exciting news, I had lost my appetite to eat. Therefore, I decided to hang in there until dinner time.

Sister Donovan asked me would it be okay for her to take me the next day at 7:00 a.m. for the denture. I nodded affirmatively with humility and thanked Sister Donovan for her thoughtful deeds. I walked away with tears dripping down the corner of my nose, reaching into my mouth where I could taste the salty tears.

I was humbled to learn how much so many people loved me, cared about me and helped me. I thought to myself: "Jerry Black never replaced my teeth as the judge had ordered him. But an angel has."

I could never adequately thank Sister Donovan for her uncommon kindness. One thing I felt I could do for her was to work hard in her class and show her how much I appreciated her by earning an "A" in her class. That was exactly what I did.

The next day finally came as Sister Donovan and I arose early to travel to Florence from Sumter. We arrived back on campus late that Wednesday evening.

When I arrived back on campus. The great news was obvious. Everyone was clapping their hands, giving me high-fives for "looking good."

By Thursday morning, the entire campus knew I had gotten dentures. When I got out of my 11:00 a.m. class, a dozen of students ran up to me saying: "Dr. Richardson wants to see you." "The President of the College, Dr. Luns C. Richardson wants to see me?" I asked with excitement. Not every day does a president of a college or university ask to see a student right away.

When I reported to the president's office. He congratulated me on what he categorized as an exceptional victory speech I delivered when elected vice president of the freshman class two night ago. He issued me a compliment on the good job that the dentist had done. He then gave me a brand new suit to go with my brand new dentures. "I think it would be a good idea to wear the suit to church and when you give another one of those fiery speeches of yours!" he stated with a slim smile.

Dr. Richardson, nodded to me that he was finished. I thank him for the suit. I then departed the presidential office with so much joy in my heart.

Later, Ms. Margaret Bailey, an employee at the college from Eutawville had invited me over to her house for dinner and for us to get acquainted. Ms. Bailey knew my family well. In eventual opportunities, she gave me a ride back and forth to Eutawville, when I needed a ride home from Morris College.

When I arrived at Ms. Bailey's house that evening for dinner, my sense of humor kicked right in—"So you had to wait until I got some teeth before you invited me over to eat, huh?" She burst out laughing not expecting to hear a joke come out of my mouth during our get acquainted session. She laughed unstoppably as I sat there with a charming smile with my new dentures.

We chatted for a few moments, speaking about the people whom we both knew from Eutawville.

When dinner was over, Ms. Bailey told me that if there is ever anything she could do to help me, please let her know.

Throughout the year, and beyond my college days at Morris College, I always revisited the campus to see her. She always carried a huge and welcoming smile on her face.

The Death:

The phone rang. It rung as though it was the sound of death. With nervous curiosity, I answered in a soft hoarse voice: "hello." It was my sister Georgetta calling me to share the unbelievable news. She said to me: "Jerry was killed and found dead in the woods." I questioned immediately, "Jerry who?" Jerry Black, my sister responded. My mind had been removed from the emotional baggage of Jerry Black that his name did not come to me right away. In fact, I always called him Jerry Black, never Jerry.

The conversation went on. "Carolina and Jerry Black's brother were walking down the road and they saw a body in the road and it appeared to be Jerry Black.

It was soon confirmed that Jerry Black had been murdered and dumped in the woods behind his mother's house.

Jerry Black and I never spoke since the night he mugged me. Although being mugged by a thug is not a comfortable feeling, I only wish a few things had transpired so that the course of Jerry Black's life could have been spared.

If I had an opportunity to have had an exchange with Jerry Black about my feelings of how he added to the perils of my life, it would go similar to what is outlined below in my letter to him.

Dear Jerry Black:

My heart went out to your entire family when I heard that you were murdered. Being viciously attacked is a horrible act. I know your family was hurt and left in deep pain when they learned of your brutal death.

I am writing this letter to you because we never brought closure to the incident when you attacked and mugged me when I was an innocent seventeen year old boy.

You never apologized or asked me for forgiveness. In fact, you never spoke to me since you attacked me in the shocking and devastating manner you did. I know that you may have been embarrassed that we discovered that it was you who mugged me that night in the dark dirt road that led me to my mother's house.

We grew up as neighbors in Eutawville, co-workers in the fish market and distant cousins on my deceased father's side of the family. Speaking of my father, this is the 50th year anniversary of his demise. One way in which I am celebrating his life is by writing this book: Fifty Years of Peril. This letter is included in the book because I want readers from around the world to realize that we should not be mean to one another, that whatever we sow we will reap and that forgiveness is an invaluable tool that we should always use. Although when you mugged me, I understand you just attempted to get some money to support your habits. I needed you to have understood that your action had a profound weight of peril on my life for many years. In that five minute incident of being mugged, I lost four teeth to a human beast and it took a Saint in Sister Donovan at Morris College to replace them by purchasing dentures for me.

The peril that I had to endure as an aftermath of being mugged was a difficult challenge for me. I would have been willing to give you my first one hundred dollars I was saving for college than for you to hurt me in the way which you did.

Mr. Jerry Black, I want you to know that I forgave you the moment you mugged me. I knew that when we went to court in the case of Black vs. Brown that you were not going to follow up on the recommendations ordered by Judge Wright. Therefore, I did not even hold you accountable for your own actions. I had put you in the hands of God. I was taught that revenge was not mine but the Lord's. I am sorry the wrath of God came upon your life. One scripture I wish you had known before mugging me is this: "What you do until the least of mine, you do unto me."

The satisfying closure to this whole deal is that on the 50th anniversary of my father's death, I am able to let the world see your situation as an example in my book of 50 Years of Peril. When others are able to read and discuss issues of violence as you imposed upon my life, discuss issues of drinking and driving as my father was killed due to someone driving under the influence and discuss issues of forgiveness as I forgive you, society can then advance in the area of human compassion and mutual understanding.

Hopefully, others would be able to see how your decision to have mugged me ties into how you became a victim as well even unto death. Others will be able to realize that it is true: "Whatsoever you sow, you shall reap."

Yours for a better world,
Byron S. Brown

Chapter 6

The Old Lady's Provocation

I can vividly recall the day I received my acceptance notice to college. I was a jubilant kid that day. The notice read: "Dear Byron, we are pleased to welcome you to Morris College for the 1983 fall semester." Being accepted into college was a gigantic victory for me. Not known as a dancer, I danced that day with blissful tears. Although off beat, I danced in hope of a bright future that will never go dim. After reading my acceptance letter several times, I went around in the neighborhood galloping with my admission letter, showcasing it with so much pride and vigor in my heart.

I was not the only one thrilled. My mother was so excited for me applying and getting accepted into Morris College. This was her alma mater. Besides, I was a first generation college student to be attending a four year college. My solo parade of celebrating and galloping from house to house came to an abrupt sprint as an overwhelming shadow of doubt rained upon my parade as the untimely words of the old lady came forth. She shouted: "Boy, you wouldn't last in college two weeks."

That did not set well with my spirit.

She began to laugh in an evil way as she uttered offenses and negative prophetic thoughts. My heart was crushed and I became furious of that old lady's provocation of my life.

Doubt had once again become a powerful force, causing me to return to a world of self-doubt, confusion and pity. The old lady's words truly hurt me. I thought that everyone would have been happy to see someone attempting to improve his life. Not this old lady however.

Her harsh words were sharp and demeaning of a person's desire to excel. It was like she took a knife and jammed it directly in the center of my heart.

A cloud of darkness fell upon my soul. I hated that I had shared the good news with the old lady who seemed to have had wicked intentions. For the first time in my life, I began to question the uncertainties of life. I became a bit more curious about the world, about people, about everything. My eyes were filled with tears and my heart pumping with heaviness and my emotion swirling like a dust storm.

I had to contend with a summer filled with times where the sweat and tears were in a race to my feet as the goal line. That marathon notion lasted quite a while on that summer day of '83.

Perhaps that old lady never came to the realization of how much she hurt me. But hurt me, she did! Why take an innocent child through this sort of emotional turmoil? This type of emotional pressure could have easily deter me from a path of believing, achieving and succeeding due to a heart bleeding because of the ugly words that came out the mouth of the old lady. At times, hearing her utterance, felt like I was being stabbed in the heart. For many days it seemed as though being stabbed would have been the more acceptable alternative. I felt strongly that, at least, had I been stabbed, the pain would have been all over that day. However, the emotional scars and perils of that circumstance lasted for years.

My lovely and humble mother and I were experiencing emotions on opposite ends of the spectrum; she from a very bright side and me from a very dark one. Indeed, Mom was happy to see her baby boy getting reading to launch upon a successful life by engaging in preparing himself in obtaining and matriculating a college education that will sustain him over time in permanent ways. On the other hand, I was beginning to cast doubt upon myself by replicating the potentially derailing message from the old lady that she had injected in her provocation against my life.

To be honest, I was disappointingly sad, very angry and quite miserable of the idea that I would be a failure in college, according to another person's perspectives of my life. Immature thoughts traveled throughout my mind and heart. The negative shadow of the old lady's provocation caused me to ponder the following thoughts: "why even bother to report to college if I am an inevitable failure?" "That wouldn't make any sense," the pity party continued.

My mother's optimistic viewpoint of me receiving a college education kept her happy throughout the summer of 1983. She was thrilled of the brilliant idea of my choice to pursue post-secondary education. In fact, she would tell her friends on the church choir and in her Sunday school classes that she was teaching at Saint James Missionary Baptist Church that I was going to Morris College in August. Mom was undoubtedly so proud of the developing opportunities for my advancement in society. Mom had wished for me to receive that exceptional education she was denied after leaving Morris College to take care of her ill father, Boston Jackson, Sr., in the mid 1950's.

Mom was not only proud of me being admitted into Morris College. But she was most thrilled that I had chosen the college of her soul and choice—her alma mater—Morris College. She knew very well that Morris College would have provided me that basic, solid and extraordinary education that will guarantee me a highly visible status in society. Mom had remembered the college's motto: "Enter to learn; depart to serve." These were some of the many reasons my admission into college brought mom so many joyful and blissful days that summer.

I was clearly not as optimistic as Mom was about this thing call "college." The old lady in the neighborhood had already cursed me, rejected a future of hope for me and laughed at my chances of succeeding in college. How is a kid supposed to deal with such frustrating pressure? How is a child supposed to feel good about his chances in life after being told "he doesn't have what it takes?" How does a teenager learn better that no one should draw limitations on your destiny? Perhaps if my father was alive, I would have followed a different path. My father would have told me not to let anyone discourage me from a path of success. Dad would have given me sound advice to forge ahead in life in spite of difficult challenges. If my father had not been the victim of drunk driving, he would perhaps been alive long enough to steer me in the right path. He would have steered me down a course of a more positive self-image and self-reliance. I believe with my whole heart that Dad would have challenged me to chart a course that I would be able to easily navigate into positive territories in my life.

I was strong enough and wise enough to conceal the old lady's rude and demeaning remarks to me. Given my predicament, I found it useless to have shared the curse with Mom. Therefore, I never told my mother about the negative provocation the old lady forecasted upon my life. The reason I did not because Mom had already gone through so much in the past couple of decades. Her challenges included within a ten-year span of losing her father to a lengthy illness, losing her husband to an automobile accident, losing her baby son to a crib death, and losing her house to a destructive fire. So, I knew at that tender age not to inflict any unnecessary burden upon Mom. Therefore, I allowed her to enjoy the great news of my college admission. Mom rejoiced outwardly as I suffered inwardly. That was my sacrifice to keep Mom happy. Without excuse, I did not believe it was necessary to interject any more pain and misery into her life. Mom certainly deserved better than that.

With all good intentions, I wanted Mom's joy to remain with her knowing that her son was headed down the path to become 'somebody.' Mom remained so proud of me for the duration of all my college days—from one degree to another degree until I received my second master's degree.

During the summer of 1983, I wrestled tremendously with my ability to excel. I had reoccurring episodes of the old lady going through my head saying with a wicked laugh: "Boy, you wouldn't last in college two weeks."

The day of illumination occurred in my life. On that day, I fully realized that there was absolutely nothing I could do in the future without an education.

On the 50th anniversary year of my father's death, I can reflect back to the past and write a letter to the old lady who could have destroyed my life with her inaccurate assessment of my potential.

Dear Old lady:

The year is now 2017. On September 23, 2017, the family will be celebrating the 50th Anniversary of my father's death, the exact date he died on September 23, 1967.

At the memorial, I will reveal my newest book, Fifty Years of Peril: One Day of Illumination that Made the Difference. You are a character in the book. I am sorry to report to you that you are unfortunately one of the antagonists. You made a provocation over my life that proved not to be true and you laughed at my chances of succeeding. As a result, your comment and laugh, played a great role in the peril that the book discusses. Let me make it crystal clear. I am not writing you this letter to make you feel bad or to condemn you (although you are now dead and as an aside, I hope you made it to Heaven).

Old Lady, I am simply writing to let you know how so wrong you were about my future success. First, let me remind you of your action, and I do fully forgive you for all your mistakes. The day I received my acceptance letter to Morris College in Sumter, South Carolina in 1983, I galloped to your house to share the good news with you. Guest what you said and did? You burst out laughing in my face and said: "Boy, you wouldn't last in college two weeks."

Once again, I forgive you of your pessimistic viewpoint about me. But here is my story. I lasted two years at Morris College. In fact, I was doing super well and I wanted a greater challenge. Therefore, I transferred to Norfolk State University in pursuit of that excellence.

You did not give me two weeks. My education has expanded into over three decades now. So long to the theory of two weeks.

My wife Joyce and the two children: Daniel and Hannah, and I are now living prosperously in the Metropolitan Washington, D. C. area, enjoying all the fringe benefits of a successful career. If I had listen to you, I would have remained living in poverty. I have successfully escaped and dodged poverty by pursuing an education that raptured me from the curse of poverty. Can you believe that I am now making more than six figures a year because I did not listen to your voice of doubt but rather listened to the voice of determination to succeed?

Old Lady, let me tell you my story about climbing the ladder of economic opportunities. You will find some of the details to be amazing and unbelievable. But they are all true. Throughout this book, the pages of my life will share whom I have become since your provocation upon my life. By the way, my resume cannot fit on one page any more. It has grown from a resume into a curriculum vita. On the road to success, I learned that education is, indeed, one of the keys to success.

In the midst of all the peril I faced since my father's death fifty years ago, I still rose to a remarkable status in society because I pursued an education and did not fall prey to your unholy words.

If you were still alive, I would say I love you and wish you God's best.

Sincerely,
Byron S. Brown

Chapter 7

College Poverty

What a mighty determination I possessed as a senior in college. I went to the extent of being homeless in order to acquire my college education. I literally spent many nights walking all night long because I had nowhere to stay as I progressed towards obtaining a Bachelor of Arts degree in English. I literally had no place of my own to call home during my last semester as a senior in college. As the sun disappeared for each day and the moon arrived each evening, I stayed up with them both during the day and the night.

I had no money. I did not have a financial system in place. The only thing I had going for myself was a very strong determination to graduate from college. I knew that the only possible way for me to escape poverty was to get my education. The thought of dropping out of Norfolk State University never came upon my path. Before any thought of negativity could develop in my mind about quitting college, there was a constantly reminder planted at the tip of my lips that said: "You remember those horrible days of dropping out of high school? You cannot drop out of college because there might not be another William James, Jr. to save you." I took heed to this sound advice and refused to ever think about quitting college. Besides, it would not have made any sense to go to my last semester in college and quit. Therefore, I had to devise a strategy that would get me through from January 1987 to May 1987.

One of the strategies I used to survive through the dark, cold and rainy nights was that I would go downtown Norfolk and hang out at the Greyhound terminal. I would sit around and greet people as they were passing through Norfolk in route to various places like Hampton, Virginia, Pittsburg, Pennsylvania, Rochester and Buffalo, New York and up into the Northwestern tip of the United States. When they left on their departing buses, the silence of the midnight hit the air. The terminal was empty with just me. I would stretch out onto one of the hard meddle seats and sleep for a couple of hours. Then, I would get up and begin to pace the streets of Norfolk until it was time for me to report to class. This strategy worked for a few nights until a Greyhound employee spotted me and said: "Hey you, weren't you sleeping here in the terminal the last few nights?" Trembling all over myself to the point of almost wetting my pants, I responded with a soft and shameful, "yes." In a harsh and very mean-spirited tone, he replied: "You need to leave now and don't come back here anymore unless you are traveling." That exchange suspended my strategy of lodging at the Greyhound terminal.

I walked away from the Greyhound terminal that freezing night without a plan of how to forge ahead. The only sure plan I had when I left the bus station was that I was not going to drop out of college. With this strong determination to be the first one to graduate from college in my family, I did not allow my circumstances to get the best of me. I was so determined to get my education. There was no time for doubt or fear to enter my heart. I built a resistance within not to succumb against oppositions of quitting; thus, pursuing the opportunity of a life time in earning a bachelor's degree.

A second strategy that I used in order to cope with the idea of not having a place to stay during my last semester in college was that I took advantage of public transportation. When I had a few change, I would catch the bus at night to pretend that I was headed somewhere and I would sleep on the bus until the bus had reached the end of its route and I would ride back down to Brambleton Avenue. In pursuit of higher education, I continued to use this strategy for a few nights.

There were many nights that I had simply just walked all night long and sleep at a variety of bus stops on the streets of Norfolk. I was very determined to get my education and I did not want anything to prevent me from reaching my goal of receiving a quality education. Therefore, I tolerated the uncomfortable circumstances I encountered along the way. It was not easy. But I realized it would not be easy for me to quit college and go back to South Carolina shy of a college degree. That would have been a devastating blow to my pride and my ambition to educate myself, in hope of escaping poverty in a world that was advancing so quickly.

One night I cleverly drafted a plan to go to a night club that stayed open until 2:00 a.m. in the morning. Since the club required customers to purchase something in order to remain inside, as a nondrinker and a nonsmoker, I felt weird. I just needed a place to rest my feet and eyes. So, I would purchase a bottle of Coke to sip on all night long. When the clock struck at 2:00 a.m., I knew it was time to begin my solo journey back to being homeless as I pace the streets of Norfolk.

One night I managed to get a place to sleep at a homeless shelter. I sleep well that night. But the homeless shelter allowed homeless people only one night without being referred. I did not bother to get registered as a homeless person because I was afraid that my application would be rejected since I was a college student.

As I began to run out of strategies, I continued to hold onto the vision of getting my college degree in May. It occurred to me one night to stay in the library until it closes at 11:00 p.m. I smiled in that adversity and thought to myself: "Why didn't I think of this sooner?" While doing that I discovered that the student union building opened at 5:00 a.m. I began to take advantage of the opportunity to stay in the library until it closed and then report to the student union building at 5:00 a.m. This significantly curtailed the number of hours I would spend marching up and down the streets while being homeless in the city of Norfolk, Virginia.

When weekend, however, came I had to devise yet another plan to endure the long hours of the winter nights. As a result, I began to stay with some of my classmates in their dormitory rooms while their roommates went home for the weekend. I endured all of this because I did not want to give up an opportunity of a lifetime—to get a college degree.

What eventually saved me from the horrific episode of marching up and down and pacing the streets is that a friend and I got a job working at McDonalds and I reached out to Mother Helen Smith to see if she could help us get an apartment. She agreed to it and we divided the rent by three. That plan worked perfectly. I was able to work and save money to buy food to survive until May 1987. I accomplished the feat of graduating from college. My two grandmothers—Jannie Lee Brown and Florrie Lee Jackson along with my mother were so proud of me. They all came to the graduation in a van driven by my brother-in-law,

Richard Taste, along with my sisters and their children. When I saw this great support from the family, I realized how proud my entire family was of and how they loved me for exercising the courage to strive in the midst of adversity.

Graduation day, by no surprise, was a marvelous day for me. I was proud of my own feat. In spite of the winter of despair, I finally began to experience the spring of hope.

Dear Mother Helen Smith,

Thank you for your many years of prayer for me. You have been there for me a number of times as I experienced the perils of life. Thank you too for teaching me to become a strong leader in the Christian faith. I know that there would have been no way that I would survive 50 years of peril without something extraordinary in my life. I am most grateful that had a positive impact on my life for twenty years— 1979 when I first got to know you until 1999 when you left the Earth for a journey to Heaven.

I truly appreciate the kind deed you demonstrated when you came to Norfolk, Virginia in early 1987 to help me acquire the first apartment I ever rented. This was a huge help to me. Mother Smith, had you not intervened on my behalf, it appeared that I would not have made it out of college due to extreme circumstances. Perils upon perils would have been stacked against me. It was truly a blessing to have a praying mother in the church and a praying mother at home—Mother Smith and Mother Brown, respectively. Both of you brought much sunshine into my life and offered promises of brighter tomorrows for me for many years to come. This confidence helped me to excel in college at Norfolk State University.

My life would have remained a sad case if I did not succeed in college. I cannot even image myself without a college education.

Again, thanks for your contribution toward my success.

Sincerely,
Byron S. Brown

Chapter 8

The Day of Illumination

Since the day of illumination in my life, I have been the beneficiary of my father's death in the sense that I never give up. Over the past fifty years, I could have easily given up by using my father's death as a legitimate excuse for not pursuing excellence or not pursuing anything at all.

I am the beneficiary of many splendid gifts. Miracles after miracles have been imprinted upon my life as a result of my determination not to fall prey to the voices of my critics. According to my critics, and there are many, I am not supposed to succeed.

I am not supposed to be that person leading scholars at Harvard University, as a Cooperating English teacher in the Boston Public Schools system. I am not supposed to be that one chosen as Clarendon School District One District Teacher of the Year in 2004, during the 50th Anniversary of Brown vs. the Board of Education at Topeka. I am not supposed to be that one whose students made the greatest gains on the SAT in the entire state of South Carolina in 2003 and 2009 and whose students had the highest passing rate on the SOL (Standards of Learning) in 2013 in the Alexandria City Public Schools at the Northern

Virginia Detention Center. But in the academic world, miracles after miracles continued to generously fall upon my life after my day of illumination. To the contrary however, according to a naysayer, these great testimonies are not supposed to happen. Rather, in the eyes of the skeptic, I am supposed to be confined to limited boundaries. I am supposed to be passive rather than active. I am supposed to be begging rather than giving. I am supposed to be ignorant rather than intelligent. The list goes on: hateful rather than loving, selfish rather than generous, bound rather than free, dead rather than living and the pattern persists of great opposite where the negative supersedes the positive actions in life. In other words, I am supposed to be that one who failed and have not tried. I am supposed to be that one who was born in deep poverty and remain in that super suppressive economic mind-set and trend. To conclude matters, I am supposed to be the tail and not the head. In the words of the Old Lady whose evil pronouncement on that day when I went galloping throughout my neighborhood in Eutawville, South Carolina telling everyone I was accepted into college, I was supposed to be a quitter and not a victor.

Throughout the past fifty years rather than succumbing to ridiculous claims that I could not do something because my father was dead and no longer living, I rejected the notion. I felt strongly compelled to forge ahead in life because I knew that Dad would want me to be successful in life. I did not go around in life feeling sorry for myself. I did not go around expecting others to do for me. I never developed the habit of dodging responsibilities. To the contrary, I was always moved by an inner force to pursue excellence. There always seemed to have been an internal compass within my soul that directed me towards chasing my dreams "to become somebody."

Ever since the day of illumination in my life, I have collected a volume of success stories in my life for the past fifty years that have been placed on the shelf of my internal walls where no one could read. Although my name and face have appeared in numerous newspapers over the years in many positive fronts, there is a lot to yet be shared with the world. I believe in testimonies. I now testify of some of the amazing success stories in my life that put me in the winning column of life:

In 2012, I founded the South Carolina Heritage and Humanities Festival, a yearly program to promote cultural and ethnical unity, allowing people of diverse age and faith to share their talents with one another. On the 50th year of my father's death, the 2017 Heritage and Humanities Festival received great recognition in the Times and Democrat paper. G.W. Hall a T&D Correspondent wrote the following on February 26, 2017:

More than 125 people of different races, faiths and ethnic backgrounds gathered to "reason together" at the Sixth Annual South Carolina Heritage and Humanities Festival in Eutawville on Feb. 18.

"This is a beautiful thing that's happening here in Eutawville," keynote speaker Pastor Henry Watson said. "I can see how this will be a blessing to all those who came today."

"These are some concerning times," Watson added. "These are times when we really need to do what this topic is asking you to do—come let us reason together—the call for ethnic, racial and political unity."

"This is a call we need to answer," he said. "Having grown up in a diverse neighborhood and being blessed to have friends of all races and different backgrounds, I know the benefits of open communication, earnest dialogues and differing opinions."

"The ability to tear down the barrier between us is to speak forthright, with respect and dignity." An Aiken native, Watson is pastor of the Progressive Church of Our Lord Jesus Christ in Saluda. He is also the current chairman of the National Church Education Department.

Keynote speakers at past festivals have included Orangeburg County Council Chairman Johnnie Wright, Sheriff Leroy Ravenell and Ernest Marcus son of Eutawville's longest-serving mayor Harry Marcus.

During his remarks, Watson asked listeners to avoid practicing the politics of divisiveness that is now so common in America. He reminded the crowd that while the United States is made up of people from many ethnic, religious, cultural and regional backgrounds, "we a still one nation under God."

"If you and I are going to be unified, if we're going to be together, then you and I must reason" together Watson said. "The more we listen to each other, the better chance to attain unity. We should communicate what we believe, but not do it in a disrespectful manner. Let us learn from the past to profit in the present, and from the present to live better in the future."

In addition to Watson, the program featured a comedy routine by LaQuitcha Lanay Washington. A native of Charleston, Washington now lives in Atlanta and performs under the stage name Lady Q. She also served as mistress of ceremonies, joking that pastors hire her to come into their churches to say things they can't get away with. Other entertainers included the "Gospel Lioness," Mekiella Risher; praise dancer Saniya Mona and gymnast Hannah Brown.

After welcoming attendees to the festivities, Eutawville Mayor Jefferson Johnson even led the crowd in singing the classic American spiritual "He's Got the Whole World in His Hands."

The program also featured the Byron S. Brown Oratorical Contest. The contest was divided into two divisions—one for elementary school students and another for middle and high school students. Contest winners were: Elementary School—Kyndal Auriel Watson, first place: Eriele Bethel, second: and Daniel Brown, third. Middle and High school—Summer Myers, first place; Kivie Norris, second; and Xavonnia Brook, third.

Other highlights included a presentation of historical facts about Eutawville presented by Herbert Sellers and the Annie L. Brown and Charleston 9 Candlelight Service. Brown, mother of event organizer Byron Brown, lived most of her life in the Eutawville area and taught Sunday school for 50 years at St. James Missionary Baptist Church. The candlelight service also honored the nine worshipers who were murdered at historic Emanuel A.M.E. Church in Charleston in June 2015.

"I am a native of Eutawville and I've always believed that, once a person has gone and made a success of oneself, we should go back and make contributions to our community," said founder Byron Brown.

"If I rose from that condition to become successful, I feel that I can encourage others to come together and use theirs skills, their talents and their strengths to transform their lives as my life was transformed through just the love for poetry, reading and writing."

Since the first South Carolina Heritage and Humanities Festival in 2012, the event has become so popular that Brown said he is considering moving it to a large venue."

The inspiration to lead such a profound gathering comes through my day of illumination. As I learn, I appreciate sharing with others. It has always been my desire to help others by giving them the opportunity to exercise their gifts and talents on the open stage of performances.

I remain grateful for the opportunity to foster a positive climate in my own life with that which I have achieved and accomplished over the years. Part of the day of illumination for me is becoming aware of ways to escape pressure one faces in society. In doing so, I often feel the need to continue to compete in society. I have already stacked and collected three college and university degrees through matriculation in higher education. Yet, internally there is a school bell ringing in my soul to always seek more knowledge, more wisdom and more understanding about the world in which we live. Therefore, I compete in applying to different colleges and universities to improve myself as a professional. For example, I recently applied to the Doctoral Program in Higher Education at The George Washington University. I was required to write an essay to make my purpose clear as to why I wish to pursue a degree at George Washington University. Whether or not I was admitted or not was the important matter. What mattered to me mostly is that I was able to competently compete with others and present a prevailing rationale as why I should be admitted into their program. Therefore, I presented the following essay to the admission committee:

I never considered myself to be an academic genius; rather, a passionate learner who aspires to excel in acquiring scholarly wisdom and applying it in ways to help others achieve their goals in life. This, indeed, has always been my mindset. My stellar performances of obtaining a perfect 4.0 at Boston College, Clemson University, The Citadel in Charleston, The College of Charleston and Norfolk State in post-graduate studies has little do with scholarship. Receiving a Bachelor's degree in English from Norfolk State University after overcoming the tragedy of losing my father in an automobile accident at age two, having my mother to run into a burning house to rescue me at age four, after having been mugged for my first $100.00 I was saving for college at age seventeen and after being a homeless student my last semester in college at age twenty-two due to poverty had nothing to do with scholarship. I simply beat the odds out of a greater determination to pursue higher education. The love for higher education was embedded within me since I was a child. One day after my composition and grammar class, my professor requested to see me. "Byron, what is your major?" "I haven't decided yet Dr. Relihan." She joyfully shouted: "Well, you are going to major in English. Your writing skills are impeccable." The next day I declared a major in English. Twenty-five years later, I am still teaching English to high school students and preparing them to pursue higher education.

I am pursuing a doctoral degree in Higher Education Administration from George Washington University as I embark upon retirement from teaching in public schools. I wish to pursue a second career on the collegiate level with a focus on African-American males attending historically black colleges and universities to pursue a degree in teacher education. My passion and experience for higher education began when I served as a Graduate Assistant at Western Michigan University teaching political science in the absence of my leading professor. In

South Carolina, I led a teacher cadet program and taught English 101 for South Carolina State University in preparing aspiring teachers. My greatest preparation and desire to work on the collegiate level stem from when I served as a Cooperating English Teacher for two years for students at Boston University, Boston College and Harvard University, through Boston Public Schools. With these experiences, I gained an extraordinary appreciation for teaching and learning. My student-teachers from Harvard, Boston College and Boston University gave me the experience to serve thus shaping minds of future teachers. Working collegiately with advisors from these prestigious universities offered me insight into the type of interaction, exchanges and sophistication needed in higher education. Working particularly with Dr. Vito Perrone at Harvard has provided me invaluable opportunities to participate in scholarly discussions, curricular design and implementation of best practices. This experience allowed immeasurable depth to me as I continued to build upon collegiate leadership participation. From 2005-2012, I served as an Adjunct Professor of Political Science at Morris College, a historically black college. It was there that my affection and appreciation for African-Americans seeking higher education grew and I planted a seed in hoping to serve in shaping them to reach their goals.

I love the Irish proverb: "You have to do your own growing no matter how tall your grandfather was." I metaphorically applied this proverb to my own life in order to grow educationally and professionally. From early on, I understood very well that I could not lean on the success of others; but I had to rise to the occasion of excelling in life for myself. As a public school educator, I have grown into an advocate to help students attending a historically black college or university. I know the struggles many African-American males experience regularly. Many of them tend to give up in life all too easily. I desire to change the trajectory of that pattern. With a doctoral degree from GWU in higher education administration, I hope to positively influence the teaching arena through meaningful exchanges of high school and collegiate connections. I hope to develop programs to promote and support black males in entering college and pursuing degrees in teacher education. I will be able to serve as a solid example of one who experienced devastating situations in life as I remind them they don't have any excuses for not succeeding. I am a living testament that education can transform lives. Therefore, I am grateful to my wife and children for cheering me on in my drive for a doctoral degree from GWU.

George Washington University is the ideal place for me to pursue my doctoral degree. Although I was named Clarendon School District One Teacher of the Year in 2004 and again in 2010 in Summerton, S.C., I can always improve upon my leadership skills. In pursuing a doctorate in Higher Education Administration at GWU, I can tap into the expertise of Dr. Daniel Klasik, Dr. Rick Jakeman and Dr. Roger Whitaker. These polished gentlemen and scholars have much to offer me from their research and interests as they align so closely to mine. Dr. Klasik's interests in student pathways into and through postsecondary education is of paramount interest to me as I pursue a field to work with students to get a college degree and become teachers themselves. Dr. Jakeman's research in discovering solution to transforming those individuals whose lives have been impacted negatively by alcoholism and other drug use is of primary concerns to me in the African-American community. This taps directly into my research interest of teaching African-American males to transform their lives from living dangerously to becoming educators. Dr. Whitaker's wealth of knowledge in continuing education will serve as a tremendous resource.

As a higher education administrator, I will seek to transform the mindset of many African-American males. I will adopt programs to teach them that it is not genius, or scholarship, they must first be concerned about. Rather, teach them to become disciplined, focused and mature in forging ahead in spite of inevitable challenges. I hope to successfully implement programs that help them to see challenges as stepping stones to success, rather than as dead ends. I will stand as a living example of Henry David Thoreau's timely words: "If one advances confidently in the direction of his dreams, and endeavors to live the life which he has imagined, he will meet with a success unexpected in common hours."

I felt pretty good about being able to compete with colleague from across the world. Being admitted into the program was not as essential as the fact that I applied and felt good about myself as a result of my day of illumination.

Earlier during the school year, I applied to Loyola University Maryland to be admitted into the Reading Specialist Program. Again, I felt that my spirit to compete helped build motivation for learning within. I also had to write an essay explaining my intent for pursuing the reading specialist degree. I wrote and presented the following essay:

As an English teacher with over twenty years of experience in the classroom, I believe the most important skill for students to master is the ability to read. From an early age, children need to be given the guidance and instruction that will help them to become lifelong readers. Their quality of life, as well as their success in a future career, is dependent on acquisition of this indispensable skill. Literacy has become increasingly important in today's world. Knowing how to read, and how to read well—fluently and critically—is vital to success in the workplace. Virtually all professions require good reading skills, and many of the more competitive occupations demand a high degree of literacy.

In addition to the importance of reading skills on the job, reading for pleasure can add a dimension of deep satisfaction and contentment to an individual's life. Reading often plays a crucial therapeutic role, offering a temporary and safe form of escape from the stress of daily living. I want my students to be prepared for the demands of professional and personal life, and I believe the ability to read well is a key step in reaching this goal. My first priority in the classroom is to equip my students with this fundamental skill, and it is for this reason that I intend to pursue certification as a reading specialist.

My decision to become an English teacher has grown out of my love for learning, specifically learning as a result of reading. As a child I was an avid reader. I loved words and well-told stories. Through books I developed insights that shaped my understanding of the world and also opened up exciting new worlds for me to explore in my imagination. Over time, as my love of reading grew, I began to feel a compelling desire to share these experiences. Eventually, I came to realize that teaching could give me a way to pass on my love of learning to others. I felt a growing passion to work with students in navigating the sometimes complex task of literacy instruction.

As a naturally patient person, I am able to give my students the time they need to develop reading skills at their own individual pace. I enjoy the challenge of helping students decode and make meaning from text. Another strength I have as a teacher is my capacity to work alongside my students, encouraging and motivating, working to help them grasp a new concept or attain a new skill. Furthermore, I believe I have a knack for simplifying complex material and for finding ways to make content material relevant and accessible to learners in the classroom. After many years of working with students from diverse cultures and at different ability levels, I have developed a sense of how to build important connections between a student's background knowledge and academic content.

Earning certification as a reading specialist is consistent with my professional career goals. My primary reason for pursuing certification is my belief that training in this area will make me a better reading teacher. Although I have many years of classroom teaching experience, I know that there is still much to learn about methods and techniques which can be used to make literacy acquisition and the reading process more comprehensible. I am eager to broaden my skill set, to learn new strategies that will make me more effective as a literacy instructor.

` As a certified reading specialist I will have more opportunities to work with a wide range of learners, both inside and outside of the classroom. Much of my experience over the past 20 years has been working with middle and high school students. At present, I teach in an alternative educational setting within Prince George's County Public Schools where many of our students read at levels significantly below grade level. These students often need intense and urgent intervention to address their severely delayed literacy development. In the years ahead, I would like to expand my instructional focus to include younger as well as older learners. I believe the task of teaching literacy needs to begin early so that the need for corrective intervention later in a child's life can be avoided.

In addition to enhancing my skills as a classroom teacher, training as reading specialist will prepare me to be a resource person and trainer for other teachers. I would like to be able to use what I learn to assist and equip other classroom teachers with the skills they need to be qualified reading teachers. I anticipate working with teachers across the curriculum to provide them with access to the latest theories, approaches, and strategies in literacy instruction.

After considering options for a reading specialist program, I have chosen to apply to the K-12 Reading Specialist Concentration at Loyola Maryland University for several reasons. First and foremost, the program is "nationally-recognized and state-approved," which suggests a rigorous, competitive program. The program offers me the preparation I need for advanced licensure as a K-12 reading specialist in the state of Maryland. Another reason for selecting this program is that the GMU campuses are conveniently located. Since I work in Bowie, it is just a short commute at the end of the school day to classes. I believe I have what it takes to be successful at Loyola University Maryland.

That day of illumination for me was the day when I was a student at Morris College and I ran for class president and won because when I gave my acceptance speech, the entire audience found my speech to be electrifying and they cheered me on from the beginning of the speech to the very end. This was the highlight of my public speaking launching ceremony. Ever since that night, I have been giving speeches breaking away from my childhood shyness. I enjoy giving speeches in public. In May 2016, I was asked to deliver a commencement speech to the graduating class at Tall Oaks High School, in Bowie, Maryland. I stepped out onto the platform and excited the crowd with these expressions:

You Did It!

To the honorees and the members of the Graduating class of 2016:
They said "you couldn't do it"—But You Did It! Congratulations!
They said "it couldn't be done" – But You Did It!
They said "No Way,"—But You Did it!

It is a remarkable feat that you have battled the odds the past twelve years while matriculating an education and you are now on the brink of success. For honorees, the reward is good grades. For graduating seniors, the reward is a high school diploma.

When you walk out of the doors of Tall Oaks High School on May 13th, 2016, you will step out onto a welcome mat that says in Gigantic Prints: Welcome to the Real World.

In that real world, you will have to immediately embrace yourself for challenges. Gone will be the days when you can run to a guidance counselor, a teacher, a principal or administrators whom you can hide behind to dodge challenges.

You will have to meet challenges head on and my advice to you will be to listen to the words in Rudyard Kiplings' poem: "If," He strongly suggests:

If you can talk with crowds and keep your virtue,
Or walk with Kings—nor lose the common touch,
If neither foes nor loving friends can hurt you,
If all men count with you, but none too much;

If you can fill the unforgiving minute
    With sixty seconds' worth of distance run,
Yours is the Earth and everything that's in it,
    And—which is more—you'll be a Man, my son!

Yes! In the real world, challenges will always be there. Therefore, always be prepared. Don't just sit down on the sideline and watch the world go by. Reflect back to the words of the great Harlem Renaissance poet: Langston Hughes, in the advice a mother gave to her son. In "Mother to Son," the persona declares:

Well, son, I'll tell you:
Life for me ain't been no crystal stair.

Honorees and Members of the Graduating class of 2016, I want each of you to rise to the occasion of going forth and making something of yourselves. When doors are slammed in your face, I want you to keep knocking. I want you to go forth and be somebody. Knock on every door of opportunity.

Be persistent in dealing with human beings. Be persistent and consistent. Keep knocking on doors when you are told no. Keep knocking on doors when you are told maybe so. Keep knocking on doors when you don't even get an answer. If you keep knocking on a door, one day it is going be opened. So, if a door is slammed in your face, keep knocking until someone answers.

Seniors and honorees, as you venture out into a world of limitless possibilities, I will leave you with an Alphabet to live by every day. On a daily basis, you must carry with you in your heart at least one of the Alphabets.

A is for Aim High—for you must set high standards for yourself because your world will be watching you.

B is for Believe in Yourself—for if you don't believe in yourself, who will?

C is for Concentrate on Your Dreams—Hold fast to dreams for when dreams die life is a broken winged bird that cannot fly. That's right hold fast to dreams for when dreams go away life is a barren field frozen with snow.

D is for Deliver Results—Be prepared to always demonstrate your best efforts because as minorities we are sometimes judged by a double standard.

Remember, they said you couldn't do it, But you Did It!

E is for Explore into Uncharted Lands—Go where no one else has gone before—do something no one else has done before. I say to You the bottom line is: If you are too afraid of exploring, then you are too afraid of succeeding.

F is for Forgive Others—Along your journey and quest for success, you will come in contact with a variety of people. Some will put forth their very best effort to get under your skin. Don't let it happen. You must be the bigger person by forgiving and moving on.

G is for Grow Strong—I want each of you to grow strong and Achieve Big. Do Big. Dream big. Yes! ADD to your life. A. D. D. Achieve big. Do Big and Dream big.

Remember, they said it couldn't be done, But you Did it!

H is for Head to the top. In heading to the top in whatever you decide to do upon graduation, always remember the words of the great American writer Henry David Thoreau: He says: "If one advances confidently in the direction of his dreams, and endeavors to live the life which he has imagined, he will meet with a success unexpected in common hours;" and to add to that, I say unto you: Never strive for mediocrity; but always go for the gusto for as long as you live.

I is for Invest into your Future— please realize that investing now promises harvest later. While we all wish to harvest plenteous, we must bear in mind that if there are no deposits, there will not be any returns. Therefore, planning for the future takes thoughtful and considerate contemplation of your dream. Invest in yourself. One of the most reassuring ways to capitalize on your investment is to smartly deposit into educating yourself beyond high school.

J is for Jump Over Hurdles—Please understand a hurdle is a part of the success story. Each life that is well deserved must be tried and proved through the fire. Genuine gold is not proven to be gold until it has gone through a refinery. Success is not success until you have experienced and conquered some hurdles. I know that you have heard that the cow jumped over the moon. I don't know why or how the cow jumped over the moon, but it certainly escaped and dodged many hurdles in the road. So, use your cow sense to jump over hurdles and jump to success.

K is for Keeping Knocking—I say to you if a door is slammed in your face, keep knocking until someone answers. Be persistent in dealing with human beings. Keep knocking on doors when you are told no. Keep knocking on doors whey you are told maybe so. Keep knocking on doors when you don't even get an answer. You must learn not to take matters personally. You must keep knocking; keep reaching and keep dreaming, until you reach your goal in life.

Remember, they said no way. But You did it, here at Tall Oaks.

L is for Listen Intuitively—Listening is one of the greatest tools any one can use to learn. Listening allows individuals to pause, reflect and meditate on a series of particular topics. Listening is the essential vitamin to a healthy career and professional life. Listening allows us to demonstrate humility in every sense of the word.

M is for Motivate Yourself for Success— Set a goal for yourself and stick with it and stay motivated until you reach a pinnacle of excellence.

N is for Negotiate with Patience and Wisdom— In the real world, in dealing with others, negotiate honestly, vigorously and professionally.

O is for Outdo and Outlast your Opponents—Success does not come to one by remaining stagnant in a world of opposition. Right at the door of opportunity, challenges and limitations will greet anyone who strives to triumph over adversities in overcoming all sort of odds.

You need to know that triumphing over adversities takes boldness, audacity, fortitude and courage.

P is for Pick up the Momentum—Keep moving forward and never stop.

Q is for Question Quantity over Quality—always do your best and never rush to impress, for the world needs quality over quantity.

R is for Remove Limits from Your Quest—Never say you can't do something. You can!

S is for Smile When it Hurts—People will do you wrong. Don't major in the minor. Stay focus on your dream. Don't let anyone hurt you to the point that you stop smiling and you give up. Remember this: Let no one shatter your dreams, your hope, your imagination, your spirit and your aspiration from achieving a pinnacle of excellence.

T is for Triumph Over Adversities

U is for Use Your Talents—for if you don't use it, you will certainly lose it.

V is for Volunteer Your Services—Always be willing to lend a helping hand. Don't always look for pay when you do a kind deed.

W is for Walk with Dignity. Keep looking up and building others up. Never look down at people. Always build others as you walk harmoniously with each other.

X is for Xerox Good Practices. Copy the positive attributes you see in others and live it. It's okay to be a copycat when you are making good deeds of others known by giving credit to the source and that you are contributing to the improvement of society.

Y is for Yield Yourself—If you want to succeed in your personal life and ambition, I double dare you to render heartfelt-services to others, by yielding yourself for a more humane world.

and

Z is for Zoom In—Now is the time for you to begin to zoom in and focus on drafting a plan for your life, for you and yours.

They said It Couldn't be done—But You Did It!

They Said No Way—But You Did It!

They Said Not You—But You Did it!

Congratulations, Honorees and Members of the 2016 graduating class of Tall Oaks High School.

You did Itttttttttttttttttttttttttttttttttttttttttttttttttttttttttttttttttttttttttttt!

So, as honorees and members of the graduating class of 2016. I congratulate each of you on achieving a level of success that each of you ought to be proud of. Keep a sense of pride for all that you accomplish in life. From time to time, I encourage each of you to look into the mirror and recite the words from my poem: "Toos for Freedom:

I am too rich to be poor.

I am too powerful to succumb to challenges.

I am too tough to be bruised.

I am too healthy to be in pain.

I am too smart to act ignorant.

I am too wise to take the advice of fools.

I am too happy to be in despair.

I am too free to remain in bondage.

I am too courageous to be a coward.

I am too ready to keep waiting.

I am too talented to sit down.

So, I will stand and be a man

While I yield to the Master's Plan.

Honorees and Graduates, I encourage each of you to go forth and be somebody. When you face the pressure of life and people try to push you down, stand tall and continue to strive to do well. Your character counts. Don't try to fight every opposition you encounter. Be smart enough and wise enough to choose your battle. Whatever you do, always do good in society, do good for yourself; do good for your family; do good for your country.

Remember, it was Mother Theresa who shared with us the wise advice to do good in spite how others may treat us.

Honorees and graduates, I am so proud of you this day. As you venture out into the world, stay encouraged. Go forth and be somebody!

With this speech, I received a standing ovation. Just as I was illuminated as a student. I wanted to expose my students to opportunity of being illuminated at this finale at Tall Oaks High School.

Dear 1983 Entering Class Members at Morris College:

Thank you for giving me the opportunity to serve as Vice President of the Freshman Class and President of the Sophomore Class at Morris College. Thank you for your vote of confidence in me to serve. I don't know how you knew it, but I always possessed a strong desire to serve others. I guess it has a little to do with my father's death. Many people showed me love along the way and helped my mother out with raising seven children alone. From the love I received, I simply wanted to replicate it back by serving.

It was indeed an honor to serve as your student leader at the college. Dr. Luns C. Richardson, president of Morris College, allowed us to grow and mature into young professionals. He was a great leader. On the 50th Anniversary of my father's death, Dr. Richardson has decided to retire after 43 years of service to the college. Time goes by so quickly. Dr. Richardson was appointed president of Morris College only seven years after my father was killed in an automobile accident on September 23, 1967.

Classmates, thank you for encouraging me and being a part of one of the greatest days of my life— the day of illumination. It was because of your thunderous applauses that inspired me and helped me to build self-confidence. Without you on that day, I don't know how I would have overcome the perils of life that charged after me like a bulldog from out of nowhere. Again, thanks classmates for help making me to be whom I have become.

Sincerely,
Byron S. Brown

Chapter 9

The Horrific Day After the Wedding

The wedding bells turned sour less than twenty four hours into the marriage. The sound of the wedding bells faded away so quickly into the vastness of the universe. So long for any congratulations. The wedding that was not supposed to even be took place anyhow. I was told that there were three things that you cannot tell a man. First, I was told you cannot tell a man that he is not saved. Second, I was told that you cannot tell a man that God did not call him to preach. Third, I was told that you cannot tell a man who to marry; namely telling him who his wife is. These were principles that I followed ever so closely as I tried to live a life void of offenses.

I had no business getting married in the first place. However, I fell under peer pressure to get married because all my close high school classmates, my very close friends and my beautiful cousins on both the Jackson and Brown sides of the family were marrying and having a beautiful family. So, in my immature thinking, I felt entitled to being married too.

Growing up as young boy in Eutawville, I did not have much opportunities for dating. There were external circumstances preventing me for doing so. I did not have a car or money to even entertain the pleasure of going out with a beautiful young lady for the evening. Adding to reasons I did not frequently go on dates during my high school days is that many days after I left school, I had to report to the fish market with my other siblings to work to try to help Mom out with the bills and groceries at home. We often worked up until midnight dressing catfish, only to rise up early the next morning to drag ourselves to school and let this pattern repeat itself, day after day, months after months and years after years.

At the age of fourteen, I joined Pastor Gathers' church. While attending Eutawville Miracle Revival Center, Pastor Gathers enforced the principles of the bible that we should not engage in sexual activities until we were married. Mother Smith, the overseer of the ministry, additionally strictly taught against a single male and a single female being out alone at night. Staying true to my faith, I pledged to save myself for my wife. From fourteen to eighteen years old I did not seriously date anyone because I was trying to be faithful to God and trying not to get into trouble with God. The church taught us to fear God and depart from evil. I fought with all the might within my soul to be faithful and to save myself for the wedding night and my future honeymoon.

While in college and away from the strict teaching Mother Smith employed upon the youth, I felt a little breathing room to escape such strong teaching. It was only when I was attending Morris College as an 18 year old boy that I began to really pay attention to how beautiful and gorgeous the girls were at Morris College. My eyes were finally coming open to the aesthetic beauty of the female body.

From the corner of my eyes, I began to secretly admire and examine the bodily structure of many of the females in my college courses. One of the females, whom I will call Pamela, caught me looking at her in more than a casual manner. She observed that I had had a half erection from looking at her and admiring her beauty. She began to blush and winked her eyes at me. I exchanged a handsome smile with her for her interesting wink. As an astute student in class, I had totally blanked out on what the professor taught that day. When class was finally over, I did not have the courage to approach her. As we departed class, Pamela looked and walked in one direction and I looked and walked in a different direction. We stepped away in shame without greeting each other.

Later that evening, I had to work on a paper for my Shakespeare class. I went to the library and immediately noticed Pamela sitting at one of the cubicles. I smiled a 'yes! smile.'

Being both, devilish and goofy, I took a seat next to her and the dialogue began.

"Hi, Pam."

"Hi, Byron."

"I noticed you in class, today;" I opened my mouth without knowing what to say.

Cutting her smile short in a playful manner, she replied: "I noticed you in class too, you bad boy." Pamela winked again. For nearly a minute, I did know what to do or what to say because her wink caused me to begin to admire her even more so.

"I am here working on my Shakespeare paper for Dr. Relihan," I said. "Me too," Pamela stated. Again, another minute expired before any words were exchanged. As Pamela crossed her legs, I felt an erection coming on. Pamela looked down into my seat and noticed I had a full erection this time. Playing it off, Pamela asked: "Do you know anything about Shakespeare?" "Shakespeare and I have the same birthday, April 23rd." I replied. "and ironically he died on April 23rd too. I get scared every April 23rd," Pamela and I began to laugh. Our laughs were so loud. Mrs. Beatrice Golden, walked over to us and said: "Ssh, this is a library."

We were quiet for yet another moment. My erection disappeared during the silence and resurrected again, when I looked at Pamela's long and beautiful legs. I got up from my seat and began to hover on Pamela's back to read what she had written so far about Shakespeare. I played Editor-in-Chief to her solo paragraph. As I continued to hover over her back and shoulders, I began to slowly massage her shoulders. She began to discern the passion that was brewing. Without saying a word, Pamela stood up, grabbed my right hand and escorted me into a dark corner on the second floor stairwell. Putting all of my religious teaching to the test, Pamela and I began deep kissing and advancing our expressions of passion for each other. So long for Shakespeare. Another romantic poet—Byron—rose on stage for Pamela.

When Pamela and I were through having fun, I began to simultaneously experience some delightful moments and emotional turmoil. I was proud because I had now done what all boys do. I was disturbed because I had violated the scriptures. I was happy because

I had gained a trusted female friend. I was worried because if anyone at my church had found out, I would have to go back to the altar and repent before the church. Finally, I was thrilled that I was able to please Pamela because she was a sweet and very kind young lady. I was troubled because I had sinned.

Pamela and I had remained friends over the years. However, time and distance ultimately separated us.

In the summer of 1991, I was twenty-six years old, already holding two master's degrees. However, I was not happy with life as a single man. With a greater desire to get married, I forged ahead. I forged ahead, however, against the will of God because I was growing tired of being single and not having any children and a family of my own.

In August of 1991, I was admitted into the Ph.D. program at the University of Wisconsin in Milwaukee. I left Eutawville to pursue a doctorate in political science at the University of Wisconsin.

Of all the mistakes of the past fifty years, my getting married and leaving the Ph.D. program at Wisconsin to pursue an ungodly relationship is the most regrettable one of my entire life.

Shortly after arriving in Milwaukee, I met a young man whom I will call Antonio. Antonio was a Christian. We quickly became friends and got along well. He helped me to get a job with the Milwaukee City Public Schools.

In my strong urge and lust to get married, I asked Antonio did he know any young lady who was looking for a husband. He offered a huge smile and told me he indeed knew someone. I asked him if she was a Christian. The answer was affirmative.

I asked him to give the young lady whom I will call Tiffany my phone number. He assured me that he will give her my number.

The next evening my phone rang. "Hello," I answered in an exciting but humble tone. "Is this Byron?" the caller asked so sweetly. "Hi. I am Tiffany. Antonio gave me your number and said you wanted to meet me." I responded: "Yes, thanks for the call."

Not known for being an astute dater, I did not exactly know what to say. However, from the sweetness of her voice, I surely wanted to meet Tiffany. I pulled a few words from somewhere out of the sky and asked: "What does your evening look like tomorrow? Mine is wide open and I am so lonely. It surely would be nice to have someone as sweet as yourself around. Do you think you can make that happen Tiffany? I am sure you would not be disappointed. Every second of your time would be worth it. I promise you if you come over tomorrow evening, when you leave, you would have something to write home about." "I can come over. It better be worth my gas money," she jokingly stated. "How does 7:30 sound Tiffany?" "Sounds good to me, Byron."

"Here is my address; see you 7:30 tomorrow night. Good night Tiffany." "You have a good night too Byron," she said.

I have always heard the phrase: "If you play with fire, you will get burned." That phrase had absolutely no meaning to me at the time. I wanted a woman. I wanted to be married and I was willing to do anything to blend in society in being a man, by being married, having a set career and having a family of my own.

I had turned a deaf ear to sound wisdom. The patience I have always had seemed to have drifted away. My ability to make rational decisions of waiting on the Lord to direct my course seemed to have also been driven away by my lustful desire to be married.

As Tiffany hung the phone up, a strong feeling of lust surged in my heart and mind. I did not want her to slip away. Afraid of being rejected, I wanted Tiffany to know that I was hugely endowed. I was a small framed man. I did not want her to judge the book by the cover. Therefore, I developed a schemed to put on a very tight short pants so she could have an immediate visual of my blessed endowment from a snapshot of looking at me. I wanted to put on the tight short pants so that my penis could speak for me. I wanted my penis to be the focus of attention and not our conversation.

The next evening was finally here. I wore very tight shorts which I bought from the Goodwill earlier that day (lol). This was my opportunity to showcase my blessed endowment. My lustful tactics had worked. Before the night was over, we had already had sex. We had violated scriptures. We had pleased each other's sexual desires. The guilt and shame kicked in immediately.

I knew that size had nothing to with love but everything with lust. The period of this sexual demon driving me away from everything I have been taught: love, honesty, carefulness, dignity and celibacy, seemed to have been a joy ride from hell.

Tiffany and I began to make sexual exchanges on a daily basis. Making out each day became a norm and an expectancy. Burning with lustful passion, I thought I was in love with Tiffany. I felt that the only other woman that made me feel as good as Tiffany was Pamela when I was an 18 year old college boy.

I yielded to a spirit of irrational thinking knowing that I was wrong. I eventually got trapped into a snare I could not get out no matter how much I tried. Tiffany and I continued to meet each evening repeating the pattern of our sexual encounters. When all the crazy emotions had been drained from my system, I returned to civility.

I realized sinning in the way in which we were engaging in sexual exploitation would only get us in further trouble with God. Neither one of us really wanted to do that. Therefore, with a lustful heart, I gently fell down on my knees and proposed to Tiffany. She accepted the proposal. One thing both of us knew for sure was that we enjoyed the sexual encounters but we both knew it was morally and spiritually wrong to conduct ourselves in the matter in which we did. Tiffany and I attempted numerous times to restrain ourselves from engaging ourselves in the sinful deeds. We failed miserably in doing so. Therefore, getting married would be the only thing to help us to correct the situation.

We had set the wedding for June 1992. However, as our lustful desires for each other continued to connect the two of us together, we moved the wedding date up to April 1992. Then, we change the date to Valentine's Day 1992. We met again, and had sex again. The wedding date was changed the next night as we both fell once again by repeating the same old habits. Before I knew it, we had already agreed on Thanksgiving Day 1991 as a new wedding date.

Excited about the new news on separate occasions, I called Mother Helen Smith and Pastor Raymond Gathers to share the news. Both of them asked me do I love her. My answer to both of them was "yes." However, I knew it was lust that was driving the emotion. Mother Smith and Pastor Gathers both instructed me to pray and ask God, 'if this woman is my wife.' I promised them that I would pray and ask God. When I was finished speaking with both of them on the phone, I went in prayer to God asking him to tell me or show me in a dream or vision if Tiffany is to be my wife.

The strangest thing happened that night when I went to sleep is that God actually answered my prayers. In my dream that night, there were three women sitting together at a table. One of the young ladies was Tiffany. The other two women were indistinguishable. Tiffany was sitting on the left. A woman dressed in a wedding gown was sitting in the middle and the third woman was at the right.

The voice of the Lord spoke to me three times uttering the exact same words, each time with stronger emphasis: "This is not your wife. This is not your wife. This is not your wife."

In the dream, I knew I heard these words coming from the mouth of the Lord. With a lustful heart, I overlooked the word of God. I excused His message to me. I turned a deaf ear upon his warning. Rather, I continued to pursue Tiffany as my wife.

My defense for Tiffany began to kick in. Every human voice that spoke against me marrying her, I interpreted it as a voice of jealousy. The people who tried to warn me against marrying Tiffany, I opposed and viewed them as direct threats to my marriage. I began to draw irrational conclusions. "They are married and have children. Why are they trying to stop me from doing the same?" I defensively wondered. I was too young to see beyond the bedroom with Tiffany.

Tiffany and I were both working for the Milwaukee City Public Schools. The wedding was set for Thanksgiving Day 1991. After school was dismissed, we went to our homes and started packing. We left Milwaukee Tuesday evening. The rain was pouring very heavily and was almost unbearable. It rained all the way from Milwaukee to Eutawville.

When we arrived in Eutawville, I was expecting a warm reception. Everyone was shocked to see and learned that Tiffany was nearly ten years older than me. Many of my family members' and friends' countenances showed me that they disapproved of Tiffany as my wife. But no one said a word. We went through with the marriage on Thanksgiving Day.

I could see the hurt and disappointment in my mother's eyes. Yet, as in all cases her entire life, she never said a murmuring word. But in the midst of quietness, it revealed that she was definitely not happy.

Now that Tiffany and I were legitimately wedded, it was spiritually legal for us to enjoy and share our bodies with each other.

Still tired from the long drive down from Milwaukee, immediately after the wedding reception, Tiffany and I drove to Santee, South Carolina to get a hotel room to celebrate our first night as husband and wife.

For my wife and me on the wedding night the legal sex began and, for my family, the legal battle began soon thereafter.

I was driving back home to Eutawville from the hotel the next morning. When I turned up into Yearling Drive, my cousin Kenneth Ravenell from Mount Vernon, New York was home for Thanksgiving, began to frantically wave me down signaling for me to stop as though some one had killed somebody. When I stopped and rolled the window down, Kenneth was panicking and told me that someone had just killed my sister Willie Mae's boyfriend in the dirt road. I said, "who James?" Kenneth said "Yes." I looked at Tiffany to observe her action. Her face was covered with nervous shock.

I did not want to go to observe James' body with my one day newlywed wife. I drove up to the house and my nephew Ricky who was accused of the murder was sitting right on the porch. I observed him carefully. I did not see any blood. Neither did I see any weapon supposedly used by Ricky. I waved at him from the car but did not say anything to him. I knew that my mother was at work taking care of my father's aunt Margaret Brown, whom we called Aunt Suee. I drove to her house, told my mother what happened and told her to get her stuff so I can give her a ride back to the house. Worrying began to consume my mother's face. We did not say anything to each other back on the way home. I was allowing my mother time to adjust to the horrible news.

When we arrived back to the house, Ricky was still sitting on the porch. Soon thereafter, the cops arrived at the house. Tiffany had become scared, nervous and wanted to leave Eutawville and go back to Milwaukee. She did not like the development of this new story.

Then, I began to hear this loud and hysterical noise outside. It was my sister Willie Mae coming from the dirt road of the scene crying very loud and nonstop. She was horrified. She was very upset with the situation. She was in total unbelief. Willie Mae did not want to believe that James was dead and brutally murdered.

With all that Tiffany was experiencing, it appeared that she became afraid and began to overreact. She started panicking and crying about the situation and wanted and demanded to go back to Milwaukee, for she had become afraid because of everything that was happening.

I could not leave my family in this situation. Since I was the one viewed with the level head in the family, they needed my support.

It was a horrible scene. My sister Deborah was crying because her son Ricky was being accused of the murder. My sister Georgetta was crying because she felt bad for James who had lost his life in such a brutal way. My sister Willie Mae was still crying because her boyfriend was now dead. My wife was crying because she wanted to go back to Milwaukee. My mother was crying because the whole situation was upsetting her. My nephew Ricky was crying because he was being accused of a crime he said he was not guilty of committing. The peril of this day drew many painful memories.

I could not leave to go back to Milwaukee. I stated in my mind: "Tiffany would just have to cry. I cannot leave my family in this mess."

Ricky was only fourteen years old. He was never in trouble. He was a very smart boy. The police officer, who took a statement from Ricky, concluded at the end of his investigation that the crime was too hideous and complex for a 14 year old kid to have committed.

In order to make sure everything settle down, I had to make three important phone calls. I called Dr. Ida Bailey and got no answer. I called for a second time and still did not get an answer. I had to get in contact with Dr. Bailey because she was Ricky's principal and she cared for Ricky ever since she was Ricky's principal.

The second call I had to make was to Dr. Cynthia Cash-Greene, a member at Ricky's church. Dr. Cash-Greene always connected with Ricky. She, like Dr. Bailey, had loved Ricky. They often looked out for his well-being. Whenever Ricky needed some special attention, he could count on them. Dr. Cash-Greene took a special interest in Ricky at Springhill Missionary Baptist Church.

I called Dr. Cash-Greene to inform her of the murder of Willie Mae's boyfriend and that community members were saying that Ricky had committed this crimes. She was shocked to learn of this new development. She offered her condolences and encouraged the family if we needed anything or any assistance, we could call upon her.

I then had to make the toughest call of the three. I had to call the deceased family and break the devastating news. When I called James' mother and sister, they were in total unbelief. They had a thousand questions and I had the same answer for each of the thousand questions: "I don't know." I then handed the phone over to Willie Mae as I had to get in contact with Dr. Bailey.

Since I could not reach Dr. Bailey by phone, my mother and Willie Mae decided to ride with me as I drove to Dr. Bailey's house. When Dr. Bailey saw that Willie Mae's eyes were filled with tears, she immediately surmised that something had gone terribly wrong. We told Dr. Bailey what had happened. She was strong, supportive and encouraging. She too believed that the Ricky she knew did not do this and felt that there were some missing pieces to the puzzle. Dr. Bailey insisted on helping the family with anything that we needed to get through this challenging time for the family.

The day after the wedding was an emotionally filled day for many of the family members. I had to divide my attention to so many people that day before heading back to Milwaukee. Worst yet, Tiffany cried all the way back to Milwaukee. I thought to myself: "What an irony, it rained all the way from Milwaukee to Eutawville. Now she was crying all the way from Eutawville to Milwaukee."

The brutal murder the day after the wedding stuck in Tiffany's head. She never overcame the feeling of fear and being timid about what was suspected of my nephew to kill James. From there, it seemed that she could no longer trust me. It appeared that she felt uncomfortable and scared that something might happen to her one day. These negative thoughts and emotions were killing the spirit in our marriage. From day one back into Milwaukee, we had a very rocky marriage. I knew that the foundation of the marriage was not built off of love but off of lust that was orchestrated by my foolishness and folly. I knew I could not live the rest of my life with a woman whom I was pretending to be in love with, especially since the murder took place.

In my heart, I conceded the marriage within the first month of us living together as husband and wife. I knew it was a marriage built out of peer pressure and lust that developed from within long before the wedding day. Tiffany and I did not have any children together. I was able to escape the marriage without additional perils of life by having children with Tiffany. When we went to court, I did not have a lawyer. I represented myself.

After answering all the questions the judge had of me, he drew his conclusion about the divorce. He stated to me: "Mr. Brown you represented yourself well in court. The best lawyers out there could not do a better job than what you did today. Congratulations, I grant you the decision to dissolve the marriage between you and Mrs. Tiffany Brown today."

Our three years of marriage came to an end. I fell on my knees, worshipped God and told him I will never put myself in that predicament again. Finally, I was free.

Dear Single Guys,

Never burn in the passion of heat. Make sure that before you pick a wife, you seek sound advice and never give into peer pressures. That will mess you up. Remember what I had forgotten: sex is never the reason to get married; love is the reason.

Learn from my bad experience and never try to grab a woman's attention because of your sexual prowess. Sex is temporal; love is permanent.

When others try to give you some advice, don't take it so personal. Understand that they only want to help you. They don't want to see you make a bad decision for the rest of your life.

Remember fishermen, there is more than one fish in the ocean. If you don't catch the best fish out in the world your first time around, you will ultimately catch it as long as you continue to fish.

Don't ignore your gut feelings, or your intuition. They are your guiding light.

Please learn of my mistakes and the perils I had to go through to overcome.

This is just a warning from one brother to another. Peace and love.

Sincerely,
Byron Brown

Chapter 10

A Widow of Faith Succumbs

She was born on October 2, 1936 to the late Boston Jackson, Sr., and the late Florrie Lee Jackson. They named her Annie Lee and gave her the nickname "Charlotte," after her grandmother Charlotte Jackson. Annie Lee grew up in Eutawville, South Carolina and fell in love with Samuel George Brown. They got married and had 8 children consecutively from 1958 to 1966. However, in 1967 her husband Samuel George Brown was killed. Dad's death caused Mom to have to raise all of us all by herself. Mom was a precious human being. At times, she seemed to be more angelic than human. She had extraordinary patience, kindness and endurance.

Mom held on tightly to her beliefs. She trained us to do what was right. She brought us up in the church and she loved all of us equally. She was a sweet and an amazing woman who never complained. She refrained from arguing, begging, and gossiping. Mom devoted her entire life to church and service. She was genuine and cooperative. One of Mom's biggest goals was to live to see her children become grown. She accomplished that goal and was grateful to the Heavenly Father for honoring her desire.

The world has always been richly peopled with great human beings since antiquity. Our mother—Annie Lee Charlotte Jackson Brown— was an extraordinary woman who should be included in the group. It is no coincident that my very earliest memory of my mother and my very last memory of a living mother carried the same message. In 1969, when I was four years old, my family lived in the rural township of Eutawville, South Carolina. One night the house that our family of eight lived in caught on fire. My father, Samuel George Brown, who had been married to my mother for a decade, was killed in an automobile accident a year and a half earlier on September 23, 1967. The last thing that Mom needed to experience was yet another family tragedy.

As the house was burning down and the wings of the fire were expanding themselves, Mom exhibited extraordinary strength. While she was in a shed dressing catfish for a man we called Mr. Hal Bailey, my grand uncle James Brown, whom we called Uncle Jug, came running frantically into the fish shed and in a panic and told Mom that our house was on fire. Instantly, without hesitation, Mom ran into the house. While she knew that my siblings Theresa, Georgetta, and Samuel were attending school at St. James Elementary School that day, she was also aware that there were four other important—very important *things* she had to rescue from the house. Mom found the extraordinary and heroic strength to run into a house being consumed with a rapidly growing fire to rescue four little children before the house collapsed from the raging inferno it had become. As I was running around in that house bare footed, shirtless, no shoes and only wearing a cloth diaper attached to my body with two giant safety pins fastened on both sides of my waist, Mom snatched me up in her arms, grabbed Willie Mae by the hands and told Ricky and Deborah to run. What an amazing act of love! What a heroic act! Love motivated her to act quickly, wisely and heroically in the moment of chaos. Mom saved our lives that day. First she rescued us and then she asked questions. During her investigation of the fire's root cause, she learned my brother had put a broom into the wooden stove in the kitchen to stoke the fire in an effort to generate more warmth.

This earliest memory of Mom so clearly demonstrated the love she had for her children. She was graciously willing to sacrifice her life for that of her children. Greater love hath no man than this, that a man lay down his life for his friends (John 15: 13). In spite of life's complexity, she was always content. There was always one amazing and distinguishing characteristic about Mom that is totally unforgettable. She never complained. Throughout all the challenges of her life, Mom endured until the end without saying a murmuring word.

Mom's last words to me two days before she died resonated the same message. When she had not spoken for a few days, and was going into a deep sleep and was only sporadically alert, a miracle happened when she awoke one of those times. As my good friend and cousin, Joseph Council, and I sat in the hospital room at The Regional Medical Center of Orangeburg and Calhoun Counties, Mom signaled me to come closer to her. After several days of not being able to talk, miraculously she spoke. Mom said: "Come here. I got something to tell you." When I walked over to her, she mustered the strength to say: "I love you." Those were Mom's last three words spoken to me. Those were the last three words Mom said on earth: "I love you." She then gently slipped back into a deep sleep.

I do not take Mom's last three words spoken on Earth lightly or selfishly. I knew that it was legendary love that allowed her to raise seven children as a single mother until her youngest child reached 50 years of age. On April 23, 2015, I called her to congratulate her on living to see her baby son reach the half-century mark. Little did I know of her approaching departure from this earthly sphere in the coming September.

The legendary love that Mom shared with all her children prevents me from taking her last three words of "I love you," selfishly. I know well enough that had it been Theresa, Georgetta, Samuel, Deborah or Willie Mae sitting there in the hospital room when she came back into consciousness, she would have uttered those same words to each of them. I believe this is the message Mom wanted me to share with all her children. Although we all knew that Mom loved us, she knew well that as part of the grieving and healing process, it would do us good to know that her last three words spoken on Earth was a personal message to each of us packaged in the phrase: "I love you." Transitioning into another world, Mom was not concerned about death, she rather chose to focus on her love for her children.

On Friday September 18, 2015, the entire family gathered around Mom all day long. We prayed. We sang. We read scriptures. We wept. Then, we prayed again. We sang again. We read scriptures again. We wept again. As the day was growing old, family members began leaving one by one, each one telling Mom "I love you." My niece Ebony Brown was getting married the next day. Therefore, family members gradually departed and went over to my sister Georgetta Kennedy's house in Bowman, South Carolina to participate in the wedding rehearsal. As the evening skies turned charcoal gray, every one began to say good night as family members planned to visit Mom the following day after the 1:00 wedding. Just before midnight, a strong feeling came upon me, urging me to go back to my mother and pray with her one more time. My cousin Joseph Council and my nephew Christopher Gadson accompanied me. When we arrived at Mom's bedside, we observed the discomfort her body was experiencing. Yet again, we prayed. We sang. We read scriptures. We wept. But something different happened this time. I spoke to Mom and said: "I know you can't talk but please repeat these words in your heart." I had asked her to repeat the traditional sinner's prayer and to ask God to forgive her for any sins she had committed or any omission of sins. At the end of this prayer, a spirit of peace and calmness came upon Mom. Her face began to glow and the hissing noise she was making stopped. The pain and discomfort her body was in seemed to have ceased. Mom opened her eyes wide and looked at the three of us and smiled. Then, she gently closed her eyes.

The next day was Saturday, September 19, 2015, Ebony's wedding day, the day that she would become Mrs. Ebony B. Sumpter. The weather was perfect. Everyone was excited for the new couple. The plan for the day was to attend the wedding and after the reception, we would all go to see Mom.

At 8:45 a.m., I received a call from the nurse. "Is this Byron Brown?" "Yes," I said. "This is Nurse… I'm calling to let you know that your Mom, Mrs. Annie Lee just passed away." I cannot recall what happened the next few moments.

When I recovered from a temporary shock, I remembered it was Ebony's wedding day and I did not want to crush Ebony's and her fiancée Christopher Sumpter's feelings. I wanted them to have a beautiful wedding and enjoy the march down the aisle, just as much as I had enjoyed my wedding day in Ghana, Africa. Mom, in particular, would definitely not want Ebony to call the wedding off for Mother herself had looked forward to the wedding. Just a week earlier Mom had inquired about Ebony's wedding dress.

With Mom's sudden death on Ebony's wedding day, I was challenged to make the toughest decision of my life. I knew no matter what decision I made I would have been criticized immediately, but in the long run I would be appreciated for my wisdom and judgment. The tough decision was do I go and tell the family that Mom had died and cast a shadow on Ebony's wedding plans, or do I keep Mom's death private until after the wedding ceremonies. I chose to keep the sad news to myself until after the wedding ceremonies. Since my Aunt Lillie Dessaure, Mom's sister, was the wedding planner, I had informed her of Mom's death and asked her not to say anything and to shorten the reception so we could call everyone over to my house on Memory Lane. The hours from 9:00 a.m. to 4:00 p.m. seemed like an eternity for me as I quietly carried this burden.

The wedding was absolutely beautiful. I had to smile outwardly with so many people while I was grieving so heavily within. But I knew my wife Joyce had been praying hard for me to keep my composure. I knew well enough that the wedding was not the right setting to reveal the sad news. When the wedding and the reception were finally over, I asked my aunt Jannie Ruth to gather everyone and tell them to come to my house. She compassionately and immediately rejected the request by saying, "No, I am going to Orangeburg to see Charlotte." Now for the first time that day, I realized that Mom was really gone." I pleaded with my Aunt Jannie Ruth to just comply with my request. Not knowing of Mom's death, she loaded her car up with family members to go see Mom, her sister-in-law. I had to think quickly before she pulled out from

St. James Elementary School, where the wedding took place. I ran to my Aunt Lillie and informed her of the situation and she called my Aunt Jannie Ruth to the side to tell her that Mom had died. My Aunt Jannie Ruth then understood what I was trying to do. She then gathered the crowd and told everyone to come to my house.

When everyone arrived at my house, I offered a prayer. Before I revealed the news, we all sat their quietly as the new bride, Mrs. Ebony B. Sumpter, approached slowly in her long white wedding dress. As she came into the living room, she had the gut feeling that something had happened. I then revealed the news, "The Nurse called at 8:45 this morning and told me that Mom had passed away." Everyone burst out in tears and shock. Someone even chanted an angry comment that I had kept this to myself all day long. I decided to remain quiet and simply let their emotions flow, for I knew in my heart I had done the right thing and handled it in the way Mom's legendary love would have expected me to do so.

While Mom lived a rather simple life filled with humility, some of the proudest moments were when she witnessed her children getting baptized. Baptism was one of the most important spiritual rituals to her. Perhaps she knew very well baptism signified an identification with the death, burial, and resurrection of Jesus Christ.

Mom had a very special relationship with God. She had the gift of vision, and she would often share spiritual foresight with her children. One such example was on December 13, 1979, we were all home and in our beds sleeping. The piano Mom had in her living room suddenly started playing a unique tune. She woke all of us up and told us that someone in the family was going to die. Within an hour, our grandma,

Florrie Lee Jackson called and confirmed the death of our Great Grand Aunt Mary Hamilton. On yet another occasion, Mom, woke all of us one night and told us that Mr. Solomon Sweeper, an elder member of the family who was living down the road from us was in trouble. She said that his house was on fire and we needed to help him get out of the burning house. We all ran to his home and there was no smoke, no fire, and no trouble. A month later, Grandma Jackson, called us in the middle of the night to tell us that Mr. Sweeper's house was on fire and that we needed to help him get out. As we ran out of the house, we saw the flames, we smelled the smoke and we witnessed death as the house collapsed on Mr. Solomon Sweeper' body. That was a sad night. All we were able to do is think back to when Mom ran into her own burning house with four of her children in it and saved all of us and give God the glory for her strength that day.

Our mother instilled within us the value to work. I remember very vividly that Mom would gather all of her children to go and pick cotton for Ms. Sarah Sumpter. In the early 1970's we all picked cotton for a penny a pound. Mom taught us to work for a living and to never beg anyone for anything. When picking cotton became a dying profession in Eutawville, our mother continued instilling within us the value of working. Many days when we returned from school, Mom would insist that we report to the shed to dress catfish for as low as eight cents a pound. Many nights when we were tired of dressing hundreds of pounds of catfish, Mom would encourage us to finish another load. She always pushed us to do more. She always told us to work hard and to always remember that it was not how much money we made but what mattered was what we did with what we made. Mom always encouraged us to work hard and to never beg anyone for anything. This is the pride she taught us and it worked.

One of the most memorable attributes of Mom is that she loved God. She loved God more than anything else. When I ran and pastored a small ministry in Eutawville, South Carolina for ten years, 2003 to 2013, our mother attended every worship service, every bible study, every seminar, every revival, every concert and every tent meeting, except for when there were services being held at St. James Missionary Baptist Church, her home church. Mom had to be there for her loyalty was unending to her beloved church. She loved God just that much and more. She always desired to be in the house of the Lord. Mom had gifted ears to hear the word of God. In Matthew 11:28, she could hear the Lord say, "Come unto me, all ye that labor and are heavy laden, and I will give you rest." Mom could hear the Lord say, "Peace I leave you. My peace I give unto you: not as the world giveth, give I unto you. Let not your heart be trouble, neither let it be afraid. In my Father's house are many mansions: if it were not so I would have told you. I go to prepare a place for you. And if I go and prepare a place for you, I will come again and receive you unto myself; that where I am, there ye may be also." (John 14: 2-3)

Mom, indeed, loved her children, loved her family, loved her church, and most of all loved God during her life span. That dash between October 2, 1936 and September 19, 2015 represents nearly eighty years of selfless living and legendary love that included raising seven children for nearly 50 years after the death of her husband. I do testify that Annie Lee Charlotte Jackson Brown lived the life of a saint and is thus remembered by all who knew her as a mother of strong love, faith, humility and perseverance. Mom never complained about anyone or anything. If she ever disagreed with anyone or anything, she would only lovely express: "Do Jesus." The special love Mom expressed was always demonstrated even on her death bed as she declared to me: "I love you." Jesus said, "As I have love you… love one another" (John 13:34). May we learn from our mother's Christ-like example, as she has loved us, may we love one another.

Dear Mom,

This poem was written in your memories. Thank you for taking care of all of us. We are so grateful to have had you as our mother. We know that if we do what you have taught us, we will not only see the Savior, but we will see you again. I appreciate all the great efforts you put forth in bringing us up. You lived a blessed life and God allowed you to live to see your baby turn 50 years old on April 23, 2015.

Many people were shocked when God called you home. But I understand. I got it. God wanted you to be with Him, because you were so precious. He did not want you to be bothered any longer with this old world. This poem is written to you:

In Memory of Annie Lee Charlotte Jackson Brown:
A Mother of Legendary Love, Faith, Perseverance and Humility
October 2, 1936- September 19, 2015

We truly miss you!
What an awesome and inspiring life you led on earth.
And for mothers, you've been one of the world's best.
Thank you for teaching us to love.
Thank you for teaching us to have faith.
Thank you for teaching us to persevere.
A year after your earthly departure and for years yet to be born,
We still cling onto that which you've taught us;
And this trend will never be forsaken by your children;
It will forever be a part of our lives and for generations to come.
Your insightful words during perplexing times,
Your brilliant illustrations of patience during the storms of life,
Your genuine guidance for us to seek truth and
To follow life's principles in the Holy Bible,
Your sweet personality that never dimmed,
Along with your legendary spirit of humility
Shall continue to exist on Earth by the lives led by your offspring.
Your spiritual promotion to Heaven is a testament to
The legendary love you shared and the legendary life you've lived.
We cannot wait to be reconnected by the Blood of the Lamb.
We have that promise that we'll see you again.
This is true because you've taught us so.
By: Byron S. Brown

Loved by your children: Theresa, Georgetta, Samuel,
    Deborah, Willie Mae and Byron
Mom, we love you.

Sincerely,
Byron S. Brown

Chapter 11

Grace in Times of Spiritual Darkness

Throughout my life, I have had numerous challenges that were man-made. However, there have been a number of occasions where I may have brought some unnecessary uncomfortable circumstances in my own life because of spiritual darkness and sin. As a result of sin, spiritual peril fell upon my life during the past fifty years. The only thing that saw me through was the grace of God. The mercy and grace of God enabled me to rise above my helpless conditions.

As I was forced by life's circumstance, I had to contend with the idea that I had to fight a good fight in order to win against evil forces in my life. Yet, I knew that as I lived in a world with much wickedness that I had to rely on something greater than myself. I was astute enough to realize that the only thing that I could rely on during perilous times was the grace of God. Time and time again, I discovered this to be true over the years.

I believed the scriptures from childhood. Therefore, I had an advantage in understanding many spiritual principles. I knew well enough that I could not possibly take God's grace for granted. Ephesians 4:7 reminded me ever so clearly these pertinent words: "But unto every one of us is given grace according to the measure of the gifts of Christ." With that being understood, I gained a greater perspective on the revealed word of God as they were relevant to my life. It became crystal clear to me, at a young age, the magnitude of God's grace.

I understood that no one has more tolerance than God. God puts up with our selfishness, our foolishness, and our disobedience to Him. Unlike millions of human beings, God looks beyond our faults and sees our needs. Oftentimes, God extends his free mercy to us. I have been a recipient of that mercy so many times. When man will not grant us another opportunity, God extends the enjoyment of His favor to us according to our faith in Him.

While concentrating on God's words, I began to understand the biblical characters who represented ever so strongly faith-in-action in their very own lives. I was able to surmise that if there has ever been a person who truly appreciates the grace of God, that person would be David, the psalmist. He never forgot anything that the Lord had brought him through. In fact, he raised a question in regards to God's extended Grace: "What shall I render unto the Lord for all of His benefits towards me?" (Psalms 116: 12).

As a teenager, I studied the bible in hope of finding some consolation in the early death of my father. I grew to appreciate the grace of God in my own life. I understood very well that through grace, God responds to the necessity of man.

Because we have all sinned and fell short of the glory of God, we need God's grace.

Grace became a necessity to man's soul, when Adam and Eve had sinned in the Garden of Eden. God directly told them not to eat of the tree of Good and Evil. Because of human's disobedience, grace became an ever needing abstract for the survival of human's soul and spirit. God forewarned Adam that the day he eats of that tree he would surely die. Adam, through his failure to obey God's order, tested God on his own word. Since that time man needed God's continuous grace.

Grace be unto God for His grace. I don't believe that there is anyone on the face of the earth who has gone before God begging for grace, a tremendous number of times as I have during my days of spiritual darkness.

During my Christian walk, I committed many sins before God. I would then plea with God each time to beg God His mercy and grace. Situations in my life would have simply been much better and much easier for me if I had obeyed my spiritual leaders, as the Word of God directs us to do so. Instead, I listened to the things that the devil told me. But thank God those days are over. When I was away from home, in college at Norfolk State University, my life was on the line with God. I became so disobedient to the Will of God and wanted to do my own thing.

The devil had me thinking that to live a life of worldly pleasure was the right thing to do. Although I had been taught the Word of God, I still could not use the Word of God to help me because my mind was so deeply buried in sin. Satan had a bondage on me. The bondage was like a chain wrapped around my soul. Because of my many sins, I became sick just two weeks before I was to graduate. I told one of my professors how I felt and that I did not want to go into the hospital. I was barred from my classes. I was forced to go into the hospital. I was afraid to go because I was afraid to hear what the doctors had to say. The doctors examined my body and took a test for pneumonia. The results came back positive. I became really scared. I told my best friend at that time, who was also a student at Norfolk State University to call my family and tell them that I was in the hospital.

Later, I was afraid to, but did, call my spiritual mother, Mother Helen Smith, whom God had used to warn me many times of my sins. I told her that I was in the hospital. She warned me and encouraged me to pray. She then said she would be praying for me. I prayed to God and asked Him to heal my body. Later, I received a telephone call from Evangelist Elaine Fuller. She prayed for me over the telephone as the tears dripped from my eyes.

During this time of spiritual warfare, I continued to plea with God for my soul. I literally begged God for his grace and to heal my body. I thought I was going to die because Mother Helen Smith, Evangelist Jannie Mae Graham and others came up to Virginia from South Carolina many times to help me with a home Bible Study. It seemed as though every time they came to Virginia, God would warn me, and warn me of my disobedience to His will. Yet that stubborn spirit of disobedience remained in my life during times of spiritual darkness.

Two days later, after entering the hospital, the doctors tested me against.

This time hallelujah the results came back negative. A greater desire hoovered over my soul to want to do better and to get my life in spiritual order. I was most appreciate that God had healed my body and extended His grace to me in a real time of need.

I was able to take my final examinations and graduate. This was a major feat for someone who had to endure the many perils of life. Upon successful graduation from Norfolk State University, I enrolled in graduate school at South Carolina State College, (now South Carolina State University). I was making all A's on my daily assignments. However, I was all too impatient to finish the summer term. So, I quit. I went home, packed my clothes, and took off to go to Los Angeles, California.

I arrived in Los Angeles, August 3, 1987. I knew that this was my opportunity to excel and to become successful. I contacted one of my former Hollywood movie star friends. He was glad to know that I was in town. I had met this former movie star at a summer Bible conference in Hampton, Virginia. Although we stayed in contact with each other over the course of several months, it had been two whole years since we actually saw each other.

He was able to inspire me a great deal. He gave up His glamorous Hollywood movie star lifestyle to become a Christian Evangelist. I too wanted to do something great for the Lord. Since I enjoyed writing, I wanted to publish a Christian magazine. He was willing to give me advice and strong support. Since he served as an inspiration, I was able to publish my first magazine. The magazine was distributed to people in California, Texas, New York, Michigan, South Carolina, Virginia, Georgia, North Carolina, Maryland, New Jersey, Connecticut, Massachusetts, Colorado, Ohio and Utah. I was on my way to a successful writing career in the Lord for I had known people in each of these states who would be willing to help me market the magazine.

Due to the outrageous cost of living in California, I moved in with my former movie star friend. We had a great time in the Lord together. We went from church to church sharing the good news of Christ with others.

Eventually, I found a comfortable place I could afford, I moved into that place. At this place, I was alone. Little by little, I began to fall from the glory of God. I became stubborn again. I did not want to listen to anybody. I wanted to be my own boss. The perils of darkness seemed to have reigned over my life again as Satan tried to corrupt my mind. I couldn't think straight. I went from one job to another job, from one church to another church and from one place to stay to another place.

I knew that God's grace was running out on me. Many times I feared the spirit of death upon my life. The last thing that I wanted to do was to die away from home.

I tried many times to get back home to Eutawville, South Carolina. However, it seemed as though I could never get there. I was too scared to fly home on the plane. I did not want to ride the bus because it would have taken anywhere from three to five days to get to South Carolina.

I was so disturbed and so confused. I did not know what to do. I felt God's grace drawing up on me. I kept saying to myself, "If I can just home to go to church I know that my soul would be delivered." I had this confidence in my home church, Eutawville Miracle Revival Center because the people there really knew how to praise God and rebuke the devil through the Holy Spirit.

One day in February of 1988, I decided to invest a little bit of money in tuning up my car. I did that. I decided to leave California to go home. When I started driving from California to South Carolina, my car was running fine. As I reached the mountains of New Mexico, the car started acting up. It began to use more and more gasoline. As I drove into El Paso, Texas, I stopped to have the car checked out. A young man looked at the car and told me the motor was just about gone. I did not know what to do or how to proceed in my journey at this dangerous moment in my life. I began to calculate my thoughts by examining all of my options. I did not know anyone living in El Paso. There was absolutely no one there that I could call upon for some emergency assistance in my predicament.

Since I did not have any friends or colleagues in El Paso, Texas, I decided that I would press my way on, in spite of the poor condition of my car. As I continued to travel, I prayed and prayed that I would make it safely. When I got to Fort Worth, Texas, the car began to stall. Ten miles before I got into Dallas, Texas, the car stopped completely. Sadly, that was the end of that car. God is grace. God is good.

I called an evangelist in Dallas, Texas, whom I had met about two years before then, when I was traveling with my best friend to his home in Tacoma, Washington. Thank God I had stayed in contact with that Evangelist over the years. He was glad to see me, but was sad to see me in that condition. He drove to Forth Worth, Texas to pick me up. He paid for my hotel fee for one day in Dallas. I counted that as a true blessing from God.

He encouraged me to think about what I wanted to do. I had three sensible choices: to go back to California on the bus, to continue to go to South Carolina by taking the bus also or to make my home in Dallas, Texas. Ever since I was a little boy, it was always my childhood fantasy to live in Dallas, Texas. Here was my opportunity. I was really confused. I did not know what to do. I decided not to go back to South Carolina because I did not want to face Mother Helen Smith and my church people in that confused state of mind. If I had decided to stay in Dallas, it would have taken a couple of months to get fully established. Therefore I went back to California on the bus because I could go right back to work the next day.

When I got back to California, instead of matters improving, circumstances became literally worst. I became more confused. I could not stand still because nothing would satisfy me. Satan had a chain of bondage wrapped around my entire body. Things became so confusing. I almost lost my mind. I knew that this was the Devil attacking me. I knew too that God was not the author of confusion. I knew that God was the author of peace. I remembered what Evangelist Fuller taught me: "God has not given me the spirit of fear but of power and of love and of a sound mind." However, this meant nothing to me at the time. For I was unable to get a prayer through to God, during this time of spiritual darkness.

I was in tremendous need to go to church to receive deliverance and total victory over the Devil. The only church that I knew where I could get total deliverance and where the people of God would work with me until I became victorious in the Lord was almost three thousand miles away: Eutawville Miracle Revival Center in Eutawville, South Carolina.

I said to myself: "I am going home and I am going to get delivered and I'm really going to live for the Lord." The thoughts of Satan immediately came upon my mind: "Byron, you better not go back there. They are going to put you out of the church and if they do that you are going to commit suicide because you will not be able to stand the pressure. You know once you are out of Miracle Revival, that's the end of you." These foolish and ridiculous thoughts continued in an effort to keep me living outside of the will of God for my life. I decided that enough was enough and that I needed to leave California and return home so I may escape further spiritual darkness.

I was ready to be delivered. I wanted to be chastised. I knew that if God chastised me that meant that he still loved me. I wanted to be chastised because at that point in my life, just to hear a word from God would have been delightful no matter how harsh the message was. I felt this way because I remembered many years ago, Mother Helen Smith delivered a message titled: "When God Stops Speaking." I certainly did not want God to stop speaking favor upon my life at such an early age.

The day came when I arrived home to Eutawville, South Carolina. It was April 1988, a beautiful spring day. That fresh air reminded me of the good old days sitting down in the back yard underneath an oak tree on a Carolina cool and breezy day.

When I arrived home, I was eager to attend church. One of the first things I heard was that Mother Helen Smith was running a revival at Eutawville Miracle Revival Center. For my soul that was good news but to the flesh that meant trouble. Since Mother Helen Smith was a very powerful woman in the Lord, I knew that God had revealed to her my many sins and my present circumstances of not having been faithful and loyal to God in all that I could possibly have done to leave a solemn and peaceful life.

I went to the revival that night. My heart was beating so fast. I did not know what to expect from the Lord. But I knew that in some form it would be a spiritual rebuke or correction. Sure enough, I was chastised. Mother Helen Smith stood up and openly rebuked me and chastised and warned me again. She was disappointed in my decision to not remain faithful to God. She was hurt because she knew she had taught me the Word of God. I was glad to be chastised. However, it made me cry that I had disappointed her again. I cried for many days because the last thing I ever wanted to do was to hurt the person who loved me, helped me and cared for my soul.

For many days, I regretted my sins and I wanted to start a new life, all over again in the Lord. God is grace. God is good.

I prayed. I fasted. I cried out to the Lord for my deliverance. When May came around, I left South Carolina to go to Graduate School at Kentucky State University in Frankfort, Kentucky. I arrived there two weeks before summer school started. I used those two weeks to get through to God. Again, I prayed. Again, I fasted. Again, I cried out to the Lord for my deliverance. God heard my prayers and saw my tears and delivered me from the situation in which my soul was entangled with the yoke of bondage. It felt like a heavy burden was lifted from my body and I felt rejuvenated as the spirit of the Lord began to speak to my soul again.

I was happy to listen to the voice of God again. I began to live a lifestyle that was holy and pleasing to Him. My mind was cleared from the corrupted power of Satan. I was again able to think, to study God's word, and have fellowship with God. I wrote Mother Helen Smith to inform her of my recent deliverance. She rejoiced with me and shared my letter with all the churches. God is grace—God is good.

I was able to think plainly again. When summer school started, I was able to study my school work without being distracted with the pressure of the world. A week later, the class took a test. Two days after that, the professor gave the test back to the students. She told the class that the highest score was 99. When I received my test back, it was marked with a 99. I praised the Lord because I was able to think clearly once again. Throughout the summer, I made A's after A's. God is grace—God is good.

Throughout my days at Kentucky State University, I was able to work in the prison ministry, the church, carry a full load of classes, and still make A's in my classes. I graduated from Kentucky State University within one year with my Master's Degree in Public Affairs. I was so happy that I could think so clearly in order for me to follow my dreams. My days at Kentucky State University were some of the happiest days of my life. God is grace—God is good. I felt that I owed so much to Mother Helen Smith who worked with me longing for the day of my deliverance.

From these experiences, it should be clear that God has been very gracious to me. One day, I was reflecting upon God's mercy as I was sitting down at my desk in Detroit, Michigan and felt a tremendous need to bow and give praises to God for spearing my life and watching over me while I experienced the perils of life one after another.

Although my earthly father was absent in my life due to his tragic death in an automobile accident when I was only two years old, my Heavenly father never forsook me. He watched over me and protected every second of the last fifty years.

Dear Evangelist Elaine Fuller and Evangelist Jannie Graham,

Please accept my heartfelt gratitude for both of you playing an integral role in my life. I am so grateful that both of you have influenced my life in positive ways. I would not be the strong person I am today if each of you did not constantly keep my name in your prayers.

Thanks for the many years of great teaching you have done. I am glad that I was a part of the youth classes you taught in Eutawville Miracle Revival Center. This experience allowed me to grow up with fear and love in my heart for God. It also contributes greatly to my being a positive and happy person in life.

Over the years, I had learned to pray my way through difficult circumstances. I am so blessed to be one of the young people that stayed on course with the teaching you have done. I often recall two scriptures that both of you taught me. I have applied both scriptures to my daily Christian walk:

Evangelist Fuller in 1979 you taught me the following scripture: "For God has not given us the spirit of fear; but of power and of love and of a sound mind." This scripture has helped me to survive the perils I faced in life since my father was killed in 1967.

Evangelist Graham, when I first embarked upon my spiritual journey in 1979 you taught me a scripture which has time and time again given me consolation during my darkest hours in life. I appreciate your phenomenal energy in teaching me words of wisdom that helped me to cope with life even fifty years after my father's death. I could not go wrong with the scripture you taught me: "In all your ways, acknowledge the Lord and He will direct your path." This was solid advice.

I thank both of you wonderful women for being a major part of my spiritual development.

Sincerely,
Byron S. Brown

Chapter 12

The Heart and Dream of a Father

I was awaken this beautiful Sunday morning June 18, 2017 by a gentle tap on my left shoulder as my daughter Hannah said in a very sweet voice: "Happy Father's Day, Daddy." I was grateful to hear these wonderful words coming from my daughter. A few seconds later, my dear and lovely wife Joyce offered me a Happy Father's day too. Then, almost immediately, my son Daniel came sprinting into the living room with a huge bag in his hand. With so much energy, he handed me the bag with a big smile on his face saying "Happy Father's Day, Daddy!"

I began to open one gift after the other. Then the most precious gifts of them all, Daniel ripped it open immediately not giving me a chance to see what it was at first. He knew that I would love it. It was a photo album filled with so much memory. It contained photos of memories that brought tears to my eyes. I had sweet memories to hold onto in June. Receiving the beautiful gifts from my wife and children made it seem as though it was Christmas in June. I thanked them for their gifts and expressed my appreciation for their thoughtful and kind deed.

I then took Daniel to Veteran's Park in Woodbridge, Virginia to play basketball. I was so proud of the moment and opportunity to play basketball with Daniel on this Father's Day Sunday. Daniel and I played two games of 21. He emerged as winner of both games as I permitted him to advance forward with the ball so he could build his confidence and skills in the game. Two people entered the court and they wanted to play two on two. We agreed to it. We decided we would go to eleven points. This game provided the first opportunity for my son and me to play a basketball game as father and son team. We were both elated of the opportunity. The first game did not go so well for the opposite team as Daniel and I won 11-1. The second basketball game went far worst for the other person and his brother as Daniel and I won 11-0.

The basketball game would have continued. However, the opposite team was speared of a third round of humiliation as Joyce called Daniel and me back to the house as we were to have a picnic Father's Day 2017.

Daniel and I rode back home to meet Joyce and Hannah outside to the grill and swimming pool. Daniel dived immediately into the pool, while I delved into the food that had been prepared. Once I was satisfied with eating, I stretched out on the long chair in front of the pool as I watched Daniel, Hannah and other children from the Meridian Bay neighborhood swim in the pool.

After resting for about thirty minutes, it was time for me to get ready for work. I went into the house and put on my security uniform, grabbed my shiny gold security badge and pinched my finger inadvertently with the needle on the badge. I got into my van and drove to Brandywine Apartments on Connecticut Avenue Northwest, Washington, D.C., where I was working as a security officer.

Once I was finished the buck of my primary duties for the day at Brandywine, I began to reflect on the day. The picture of my father flashed before me.

The pain of not having a father in my life resurfaced. I thought about all the agony and pain that I suffered during the fifty years since my father died. I felt cheated in life knowing that I would have been a far better person in life had my father lived and not died in an automobile accident due to the hands of a DUI—a person driving under the influence of alcohol.

I pondered the thought of how my life would have been different if my father was alive.

I thought about how I never had the opportunity to play ball with my father as I was playing ball with my son Daniel.

I thought about how I serve as a husband, father and protector and I did not even have the opportunity to experience life from this window with my father. His life was cut all too short. Nothing erases the thoughts of how life would have been different for my siblings and me had Dad lived a full life on this earth.

One thing that Dad's death has encouraged me to do is to be the best father to my children. Never once do I desire Daniel or Hannah to suffer in any way unnecessarily. I want them to encounter the best experiences life has to offer them. I don't want Daniel and Hannah to have to experience the economic hardship that I had to experience growing up in Eutawville, South Carolina. Rather, I desire for them to be exposed to fresher and richer ideas about our world's economy.

In an effort for Daniel and Hannah to escape future poverty, I teach them the value of money. Each time I give them an allowance, I remind them that they must put something into their bank accounts. I opened a bank account for Daniel and Hannah shortly after they were born. By the time Daniel was five, he had already made so many teller friends in the bank. One day when Daniel was five years old, he had deposited some money in the bank, received his receipt from the teller, and turned around to someone walking in the bank. Daniel responded: "Welcome to Bank of America." Everyone in the bank thought that was so humorous coming from a five year old child. The point here is that Daniel and Hannah have received early opportunities to forge ahead in life. Just a two minute experience in the bank helps children to build self-esteem at an early age. The self-esteem, within itself, will enable children to become productive members of society in future years. They will be able to make economically sound decisions that will impact their lives for generations to come.

Some of the perils, I faced as a child and even as a young adult could have easily been avoided in my life, if I had the presence of a father in the home to serve as a role model for me. In fact, it seems as though I encountered perils in my life even more so as a result of growing up in a single parent home. If my father had been alive while I was growing up, he would have no doubt influenced me in a positive manner to live life with kindness, dignity and a spirit of optimism towards success and achievements.

Dear Daniel and Hannah:

Please know that you are blessed to have a father in your lives. A real father will always be there for you know no matter what you may experience in life. I was not as fortunate as you two are. My father was not present in my life due to his tragic accident when I was just two years old. That was a devastating blow to the family's structure. However, I did not use my father's death as an excuse for not succeeding in life. In fact, it was the contrary. Because my father was not alive, I felt the need to push forward so that I could avoid poverty in the future.

As your father, know that I have made plans for you. I am here for you. I have opened up savings accounts for you. I have purchased land for you. However, please do not become complacent in life. Go out and succeed. Write your own success story.

You have the potential to excel and become two of the greatest world leaders. Don't sit back and watch the world go by. Instead, use your skills, your intelligence and your talents to forge ahead in life.

Daniel and Hannah, I am proud to be your father. Remember, I did not have a dad and I made it. With this in mind, I am sure that you will realize your dreams in time.

Daniel and Hannah, I love you!

Sincerely,
Byron S. Brown

Chapter 13

Advice for Fathers Now and Fathers to Be

In order for fathers now and fathers to be to avoid many perils in their lives, in this chapter, I wish to consolidate some of the great quotes, messages and aspirations by others who share visionary leadership for manhood and fatherhood. In doing so, I wish for each man that reads this book to become cognizant of the power within that progressively shapes and forms a person into living life to the fullest in a most positive manner.

1. I believe that what we become depends on what our fathers teach us at odd moments, when they aren't trying to teach us. We are formed by little scraps of wisdom.

    Umberto Eco

2. I cannot think of any need in childhood as strong as the need for a father's protection.

    Sigmund Freud

3. A good father is one of the most unsung, unpraised, unnoticed and yet one of the most valuable assets in our society.

Billy Graham

4. The power of a dad in a child's life is unmatched.

Justin Ricklefs

5. One father is more than a hundred schoolmasters.

George Herbert

6. I talk and talk and talk, and I haven't taught people in 50 years what my father taught by example in one week.

Mario Cuomo

7. The imprint of a father remains forever on the life of the child.

Roy Lessin

8. Nothing has brought me more peace and content in life than simply being a good husband and father.

Frank Abagnale

9. Being a father has been, without a doubt, my greatest source of achievement, pride and inspiration. Fatherhood has taught me about unconditional love, reinforced the importance of giving back and taught me how to be a better person.

Unknown

10. Being a great father is like shaving. No matter how good you shaved today, you have to do it again tomorrow.

Reed Markham

Here are eight principles for Parenting Tips for Dads: Being an Engaged, Supportive and Loving Father

Unknown

• Spend time with your child . . .
• Discipline with love and positive parenting . . .
• Be your child's role model . . .
• Earn the right to be heard . . .
• Be your child's teacher . . .
• Eat together as a family . . .
• Read to your child . . .
• Respect the other parent of your child.

Dear Fathers and Fathers to Be:

Children are a blessings to a family. Love your children. Love is the cement for a relationship that will be reciprocal. Children are aware of the fact whether they are being loved or mistreated. Be a good role model. Our lives are constantly being watched and observed by our children. They develop positive self-esteem when they perceive that they are being treated with special love and care. They respond beautifully to such passionate and awe-inspiring moments.

We are living in a society where technology can be our greatest blessings and at the same time can be our worst curse in rearing children. We must be able to find that balance in allowing our children to use technology for educational purposes and limited and monitored entertainment. Please use wisdom in applying advanced technology with the children.

Teach the children financial responsibility early on. Open a bank account for them and help them to keep their own balances as they purchase items they want. This teaches them the value of money and how to save.

Spend time with your children. Go for healthy walks. Read to them or have them read to you every day. Have fun and enjoy them. Discipline them with love and avoid destroying their hope and enthusiasm for anything. Pray with your children and help them to recognize that there is a higher being in the universe. Teach them to respect adults by being respectful to our wives or significant others.

Be a good father. Be a virtuous father. Be an inspiring father and watch your children grow to become your greatest pride and joy.

Sincerely,
Byron S. Brown

Chapter 14

Fifty Years of Sound Advice: 1967-2017

Five decades of perils employed upon a person's life may seem to be very devastating. While I have had more than my share of ups and downs in this life, I still hold onto the faith and hope that I will one day again see my father, my mother, my grandparents and all the love ones that I have lost over the past half of a century.

In true honor of my father's 50th anniversary death date, I envision from my father that he would want me to live a life that is pleasing in both the sight of God and man. I understand my father to be a man of integrity. He was a man with a big sense of humor. He also feared God. Expressed in this chapter is a collection of good thoughts that any father would want to pass on to their children. These reflections come from a variety of conferences talks for the past fifty years from 1967- 2017. I know that my father would be so proud if I were to take these profound statements to live by.

The advice presented in this chapter comes mostly from the conference talks from the Latter-Day Saints Church. This is not an endorsement of the church but a recognition of the quality and meaningfulness of their conference talks. Following each statement is my own personal responses and reflections to the yearly presentations.

All the quotes that are highlighted in this chapter will help anyone to avoid, cope or conquer the perils he or she might face in life. I prioritize each of these statements as the quote of the year. All the conferences talk quotes come from the April General Conference because April is the month I was born.

1967 Quote of the Year:

> *"Everything is copasetic."* *Samuel George Brown*
>
> I was told that every time my father was asked how things were, he would respond: "everything's copasetic." This reveals a lot about my father's viewpoints on life. It shows a positive reaction to life's circumstances. He did not allow the pressure of life to weigh him down. I could only image my father being a very happy person who did not allow anything to bother him. I must say that I have adapted this strong characteristic from my Dad as I always looked upon life from a brighter and most optimistic lens. 1967 was the year my father was killed.

The message here is for us as human beings is to be content no matter what is happening around us.

1968 Quote of the Year from "Strength to Love" by Dr. Martin Luther King, Jr. 1968 was the year Dr. Martin Luther King, Jr. was assassinated.

> *"The ultimate measure of a man is not where he stands in moments of comfort and convenience, but where he stands at times of challenge and controversy."*
>
> This is a beautiful quote that speaks volume of the stature of a real man, or a strong person. It is very easy for people to go along with a plan as long as everything is going well. For example if everything is copacetic, people will stick around and the crowd grows bigger as people may enjoy themselves in a variety of ways. When things are peaceful and quiet, it is easy to assemble ourselves and agree on many issues and concerns. However, when the table is turned, it becomes a major challenge for people to get along or to come into agreement with each other. This ought not to be. What Dr. Martin Luther King, Jr. is simply reminding us here and implying is that one can determine a person's strength by how he responds to conflicting circumstances in life.

The message here is for us to be strong and vigilant at all times.

1969 Quote of the Year "Intention to Put A Man on the Moon" by President John F. Kennedy

"I believe that this nation should commit itself to achieving the goal before this decade is out, of landing a man on the Moon and returning him safely to the Earth."

President Kennedy knew it would be a major milestone to put man on the moon. Yet, he hoped that this would have been accomplished before the decade of the 1960s ended. He also knew that this would make two huge statements. One would be that America has accomplished a feat that no other nations has succeeded in at that time. Also, it would have solidify that America, indeed, is a great country. The goal here was not only to place man on the moon, but to also usher man back to America safely. It should be understood here that President Kennedy was a dreamer and one who put wings to his dreams.

The message here is for us to not just image something magnificent happening but to make something magnificent happen.

1970 Quote of the Year from "Goodread" by Maya Angelou

> *"There is no greater agony than bearing*
> *an untold story inside you."*
>
> Dr. Maya Angelou was not only one of America's most celebrated poets but one of the universe's best poets in the history of the world. She was well-respected worldwide for her gift as an artist. This quote urges everyone to recognize within themselves that there is a story hidden somewhere in the deep core of the human soul. This quote pushes one to unearth the story that remains yet untold within oneself. She concludes that it must be agonizing to keep something so powerful to yourself. Within this book, I have shared some stories for the first time that occurred during the past fifty years. That is a long time to be in agony. After fifty years of peril, I found it necessary to pass my story on to the world. Maybe through the words of my testimony, somebody might get to know themselves better by writing the story of his or her life.

The message here is for each person to become inspired individuals to write his or her own story so that others may benefit from the challenges exposed.

1971 Quote of the Year from "Be Slow to Anger" by ElRay L. Christiansen

> *"We are constantly exposed to irritations as we mingle with others—and even when we are alone. How we react to these irritations is a reflection of our personalities and temperaments. It would seem reasonable to believe that in order to develop a healthy, pleasing personality and to become useful and an influence for good, one must avoid being easily provoked to anger."*

As human beings, it appears that more often than not that our resolves are constantly being challenged. We must come to the realization that people may sometimes treat us with great disrespect. The challenge remains that it does not matter how badly a person irritates us. What truly matters is how we react to how we are being treated. Sometimes such irritation comes in the form of a test for us: testing our patience, testing our faith, and testing our kindness. Wise counselors have warned us that if we fail one of life's tests, we must continue to take that same test again and again until we have succeeded. Therefore, as the actions of others provoke us, we must remain mindful that we cannot succumb to their folly. Rather, we must resist the irritable nuances and stand perfectly clear away from retaliating against others. We must be the epitome of something greater than those who travel the low road. Yes, we must stay on the high road, even in the midst of adversities. We cannot allow ourselves to become provoked under any circumstances.

The message here is for us to be humble, grateful, strong and vigilant at all times to avoid the snares of the adversary on any given day.

Byron S. Brown

1972 Quote of the Year from "Keep the Lines of Communication Strong" by Spencer W. Kimball

> *"We are too affluent. We have too much money and other things. We have so many things. Even many poorer people have many things, and "things," become our life, and our vocabulary has been invaded with, 'Let me do my thing."*

It is biblically stated that "the love of money is the root of all evil." The bible also offers the analogy that it is harder for a rich man to enter into heaven than for a camel to go through the eye of a needle. This is certainly without exaggeration. While it is desirable for all of us to be rich and not poor, prosperous and in good health, not having the right foundational teaching on the principles of spending and budgeting may cause us to experience some rather prideful spending that results in ugly turnovers. Money has become less scarce in recent years. Our belongings is now a major surplus for many of us in many areas of our lives. When I was growing up in the 1960s, I barely owned a decent pair of shoes. Today, I have to debate which pair of shoes best goes with which shirt, and which pants, and which tie and yes, even which pair of socks. However, the abundance of material items does not make a person rich. What makes a person rich is one who has the basic necessity of life and invests into "things" that can improve his or her life. Investing is the key: investment in education, investment in spending time with family, and investment with planning a future that promises hope and fulfillment in the years to come are ideal situations which lead to a good life over a glamorous lifestyle. If not properly applied, too much wealth can push people in a direction that is self-defeating and self-detrimental.

The message here for us is to not let anything separate us from righteous doing to our families, our friends and ourselves.

1973 Quote of the Year from "Consider Your Ways" by L. Tom Perry

"Our unconquered appetites and consuming drive for material possession appear to be leading us on a course so often repeated in history: Greed, lust, and desire historically have only led mankind to waste, destruction and suffering."

Out of control spending and out of control consumption place us in a dangerous position in society. We must regain control of our natural appetites. Too much of anything allows us to become hoarders thereby cluttering not only our physical space but our mental space as well. Oftentimes, we purchase things we don't need. We spend just because we have it to spend. We become unconsciously wasteful because we enjoy being in the state of having. We become vulnerable to the idea that the more we have of something, we are better off. I was told a long time ago that 'less is more.' That thought confused me until I came to the realization that when I had less, I appreciated things more.

If we are not careful, we could cause our assumed richness to cause us to lose grip on the reality to save and stay on course of living within our boundaries.

The message here for us is to not be wasteful and destructive in the natural or the spiritual.

1974 Quote of the Year from "Parents Teach Your Children" by Paul H. Dunn

> *"Too often it is easier to criticize, to point out the faults, than to praise or give love. Mothers and dads, when was the last time you told your children 'I love you'?"*

Human beings have a tenacity to focus more on the negative than the positive. If a person does something extraordinarily pleasing, it does not immediately make it into the newspaper. However, the minute a person does something wrong, it is highlighted to the greatest extent of the law. This is partly so because bad news sells and good news take a back seat during the time of the controversial situation. I have also noticed over the years that people tend to be overly critical and quick to point out the faults of others. How much stronger would this world be if we all simply demonstrated compassion one for another? As parents, we are quick to jump on the children for the first thing they don't do right. We must remember that we too were once young and naive and foolish. We were not always perfect. In fact, we have never been perfect. Then, why is it that we expect others to be perfect? We must all begin to give a little tender loving care to others. Our children need to hear from us that we love them. If they don't feel love from us, they will go other places seeking love. I tell my children every day that I love them. When was the last time you told your children that you love them?

The message here is that love is the cement to building a great relationship with our children that would last throughout a lifetime.

1975 Quote of the Year from "Success is Gauged by Self-Mastery" by N. Eldon Tanner

> *"The height of a man's success is gauged by his self-mastery, the depth of his failure by his self-abandonment. And this law is the expression of eternal justice. He who cannot establish dominion over himself will have no dominion over others."*

We all have the potential to be successful. How successful we become is up to us. Self-reliance, then, becomes a major factor in our efforts to succeed in this life. We must become disciplined individuals in order to reach a pinnacle of excellence in our endeavors. We must believe in our ultimate potential in order to strive smoothing into a world that is filled with lucrative opportunities. It is of paramount importance that we delve into the inner part of our imagination and exercise our wisdom and talents in such a manner that we promote and produce strategies to excel in whatever endeavors we pursue in this life.

Self-control and self-mastery are nonnegotiable ideals when it comes down to planning a path to true success in the world. It is imperative, then, that we yield ourselves to achieving excellence by modeling for others to follow and emulated our steps. We must provide examples for the rest of the world by demonstrating mastery in our own lives. Once we do this, we are able to help others find clearer and smoother path to success.

The message here is that we ought to first show signs of strength and resilience in our own lives before we can help others to conquer their fears of succeeding in life.

1976 Quote of the Year from "The Stone Cut without Hands" by Spencer W. Kimball

> *"If you wish to get rich, save what you get. A fool can earn money, but it takes a wise man to save and dispose of it to his own advantage."*

When I was a little boy, I was taught to save. Mom used to say: "Save your money for a rainy day." My grandfather used to say: "It is not how much money you make, it is what you do with what you have." My uncle Richard used to say: "Don't hang out with folks who don't have anything because you will be just like them. Hang out with someone who has something and you will have something." As I was growing up, it seemed like everyone liked and echoed a famous line from Billie Dee Holiday: "Mama may have. Papa may have. But God blesses the child who has his own." I could not escape the many messages of saving when I was growing up. Although I grew up in poverty, instilled within me was the desire to want to be somebody and to excel in life. Excelling in life, for me, was equated to not having to live in poverty. I was surrounded by family members who wanted to do well. I adopted the habit of saving as a part of my strategy to escape poverty. The mere fact that I saved my first $100.00 for college in the early 1980s speaks volume of my desire to resist poverty in the years to come. Money does not buy happiness, but it surely eases the agony of not having and lacking the necessities of life.

The message here is that we should be good stewards of our own money and to always have something set aside just in case of an occurrence of natural hardship and unforeseeable circumstances.

1977 Quote of the Year from "Integrity" by N. Eldon Tanner

> *"We need more integrity in government. We need to be governed by men and women who are undivided in honorable purpose, whose votes and decisions are not for sale to the highest bidder. We need as our elected and appointed officials those whose characters are unsullied, whose lives are morally clean and open, who are not devious, selfish, or weak. We need men and women of courage and honest convictions, who will stand ready to be counted for their integrity and not compromise for expediency, lust for power, or greed; and we need a people who will appreciate and support representatives of this caliber."*

If you would like to participate in changing the course of society, you should always cast your vote. Voting allows you to make a statement. Rather than complaining about circumstances and situations that may never change unless it reaches the table and ears of those in power, your work is in vain. When choosing a candidate, we must not just vote with a particular party because that is the one in which we were born. We must consider that position of each candidate. We must have the courage to inform as well as support our elected officials both in the good times and the challenging times.

Voting is a constitutional right and to participate in exercising that right is a marvelous opportunity to express yourselves. For many people, voting is a privilege that was denied early on. As 2018 rolls in, the rights for women to vote will only be the 100th year. Putting this in perspective, when my father was killed fifty years ago, women were only voting for 49 years prior to that tragic day of September 23, 1967. Historically, African-Americans were not even allowed to vote because we were considered properties. Under these circumstances, I cannot understand how people can sit home and not go out to vote. Election Day is your opportunity to voice your opinion. Therefore, make sure that you begin to engage yourselves in civil participation every time that you get a chance to do so from now on.

The message here is to realize that you have the power to elect men and women of courage and honest convictions who stand ready to fight for you with dignity and respect.

1978 Quote of the Year from "No time for Contention" by Marvin J. Ashton

> *"Our is to conscientiously avoid being abrasive in our presentations and declarations. We need constantly to remind ourselves that when we are unable to change the conduct of others we will go about the task of properly governing ourselves."*

It is human tendency to find faults with others, rather than to work on ourselves. We must begin to conduct self-reflections on ourselves. We are all familiar with the analogy that if we point one finger at someone, four more fingers are being pointed towards ourselves. When we conduct self-inventories, we learn so much about ourselves. I remember one day, I gave my students a journal topic that caught their attention: "What is it that you like most about yourself?" One of the students shouted: "Mr. Brown, I really like this topic. Most of you topics are boring." I immediately responded, "Excuse me?" The student laughed and looked at me with trying to clean the statement up, "You know what I mean. I like this topic. It is interesting like the rest of your journal topics." "Okay, Brian, do your work," I ended the conversation. Internal evaluations of who we are should be a regular routine. When we do self-reflection, we are able to grow and mature into a much stronger person. We need not continue to judge others. But we must prepare ourselves to become the best possible individuals we can become. We cannot change anyone else. When can only changes ourselves.

The message here is that the more self-reflections we do, the better we become as individuals in the long run, meaning we are better able to serve humanity.

1979 Quote of the Year from "This Is a Day of Sacrifice" by Ezra Taft Benson

> *"If you would find yourself, learn to deny yourself for the blessings of others. Forget yourself and find someone who needs your service, and you will discover the secret to the happy, fulfilling life."*

This quote teaches us to learn how to deny ourselves of certain things in life in order to help other. We are urged to help others. When we put our needs behind us and reach out to help others, we begin to live a selfless life. When we bless others, we must not look for them to pay us for the service we render to them. Help them and forget that you have helped them.

The second portion of this quotes encourages us that we will find ourselves to be happy when we bless others.

When we do bless others, we should not hold that blessing over their head and constantly remind them of what you have done for them. Have you ever heard someone being described as a person who will give you the shirt off of his back? That is probably the type of person who will always be happy. This person will have a happy life, because he has satisfied the need of some people.

We must remember the theme of the least of these. Christ has shared his views on giving. He notes: "What you do unto the least of mine, you do unto me."

"The message here is for us to deny our fleshly desire and sacrifice to help those who are less fortunate."

1980 Quote of the Year from "No Unhallowed Hand Can Stop" the work by Spencer W. Kimball

> *"Let us, then, press on confidently in the work of the Lord as we look forward to the glorious years of progress ahead. Through our faithfulness, all that God has promised will be fulfilled. This is the work of the Lord. The gospel is true."*
>
> Here we are encouraged to keep our faith in God. There will be many hardships. But we must be willing to endure. Because if we endure the trials of life and the many temptations that come our way, we will ultimately be blessed in due season.
>
> In staying on course, spiritually, there will be ample opportunities for blessings to come back our way. We must not take a detour from God's word. We must endure like a good soldier.
>
> As we press forward with confidence, we can be assured as we are being led the spirit of the Lord, we will be able to make strides both spiritually and naturally.

The message here is not to be unfaithful and never give up in life.

1981 Quote of the Year from "The Dignity of Self" by James E. Faust

> *"The desire for profitable gain and popularity in the entertainment world has unmasked in the most appealing way all of the evils of the human race. The most revolting practices and perversions have been masqueraded and even urged upon our inexperienced young people by some seeking to seductively merchandise the evil side of human behavior. Consciences seem seared with a hot iron, spiritual cells seem closed. Ideals of emptiness and uselessness of life are fostered. Nobility of thought and purpose seem not to be sufficiently taught, encouraged, or valued."*

Human beings sometimes have the tendency to put money first and then all other things follow. This is becoming a sad and ridiculous trend in our society. Values are not being taught in the home on a regular basis.

Money has, in some cases, caused separation in many relationships. Some marriages even comes to an abrupt ending because of how the evil intent of money gets in the way of love, trust and respect. Some people have even gotten to the point where they idolize money, worship money and has place money as a top priority in their lives. While there is absolutely nothing wrong with being wealthy, and we all desire to be wealthy, we must not let money rule our consciousness.

We can no longer let 'ideals of emptiness and uselessness of life be fostered. Indeed we most revisit the theory of money usage and do something differently. I believe that James E. Faust has the right answers to our concern here. He strongly suggests that we must once again begin to teach values. He specifically notes: "Nobility of thought and purpose seem not to be sufficiently taught, encouraged and valued."

The message for us here is to reexamine ourselves and our practices in order to reprioritize our values bearing in mind that money is not everything.

1982 Quote of the Year from "We Believe in Being Honest" by Mark E. Petersen

> *"Christ is our all, and without Him we are nothing. Honesty, truth, virtue, and kindness are hallmarks of true Christianity. If we lack them, we can hardly say that we follow Christ."*
>
> It is well-noted here that if we have Christ in our lives, we have everything. If we do not have Christ in our lives, we don't have anything. I don't believe that that could be put more accurately that that how it is already stated. Everything we need and everything that we will ever need is in Christ.
>
> As we live our lives from day to day, there are some expected norms that must be exhibited in our lives. Let us examine some of those characteristics. If we are not honest with our fellow-man, can we truly be a Christian? If we are not truthful, can we claim to be living a life that is pleasing to God and mankind? If we have no virtue, can we call ourselves Christians? If we are not kind one to the other can we say that we are being obedient to the scriptures?
>
> There has to be some defining features and characteristics that help us to demonstrate the love of Christ in our daily walk. In order to make the world a better place, we must exercise the qualities of being honest, truthful, virtuous and kind-hearted to one another.

The message for us here is to demonstrate the love of God to one another at all times.

1983 Quote of the Year from "Unity" by Marion G. Romney

> *"There is but one way that we can be united, and that way is to seek the Lord and his righteousness. Unity comes by following the light from above. It does not come out of the confusions below. While men depend upon their own wisdom and walk in their own way, without the guidance of the Lord they cannot live in unity. Neither can they come to unity by following uninspired men."*

This passage calls for us to be united. We all know the power of coming together. Yes, we are stronger in numbers. If we are all operating on the same page spiritually, we can improve the quality of the world in which we live.

There are several advantages of walking together in unity. When we walk together, we can achieve more together in our society. Think about a person's job in any company. One person alone does not make the business shine. Rather, when team efforts are put in place, more is accomplished.

We are discouraged from depending on our own ideals to get something accomplished. Rather, we are simply encouraged to bring our skills and our talents under one roof and let us make a difference in society.

The message for us here is to become unified in our vision to inspire others as we seek world peace.

1984 Quote of the Year from "A Generation Prepared to Make Wise Choices" by Elaine A. Cannon

> *"We must raise up a generation that is prepared to make wise choices, to stand and to withstand."*

As adults, we must be examples for the younger generation to follow. We must have standards taught in our homes, our schools, our churches and our communities in raising children. We cannot sit back and watch our youth fall into a pit hole. We must teach them to do the right thing in society.

When my grandmother, Florrie Lee Jackson, turned a hundred years old on August 15, 2011, I asked her what does she think contributes to her long life. She responded: "Just treat everyone right and mind your own business." We must concur that treating every one right is a wise choice. We must also agree that mind our own business too is a wise choice.

None of us have to have a Ph.D. in order to make wise decisions. We must discover new ways to tap into the spirit of the young generation. It becomes our responsibility, as adults, to teach the youth how to make wise decisions so that they may be able to stand and fight against all odds. We must prepare them to make wise decisions not only for today; but also for many tomorrows of the future where they will become the senior citizens of the world.

The message for us here is to pass on a legacy of wise teaching to the younger generation so that they may excel in all their endeavors.

1985 Quote of the Year from "The Joy of Service" by F. Arthur Kay

"My earnest desire is to kindle in their hearts that which burns so deeply and strongly within my own, that they, too, may have the peace, the happiness, the security, and the spiritual strength that gospel living brings."

Peace, happiness and security are virtues we all wish to experience. It is a wonderful concept to have peace among all men. When we are peaceful, we can overcome the fears of the world and begin to move toward achieving unity across the board of all racial lines. The bible teaches us to have peace among all men. Specifically, it states: "Follow peace with all men." As we yield to the peace of God, our souls will always be confidently assured in Him.

Happiness is what we all should experience in our lives. By doing the right thing, or making smart choices in life, we avoid much negativity and unhappiness. We must remember that the joy of the Lord is our strength. When we are happy, we make better choices in our lives. It is only when we are sad and miserable that we are not able to think righteously, rationally or rightfully.

When we elect to serve God with our whole heart, God will protect us at all times. When one chooses to follow Christ, he will always be protected. God will shield and protect His own from any danger or calamities.

The message for us here is to know that 'no weapon that is formed against us shall prosper against us' at any time no matter how stiff the challenges may be.

1986 Quote of the Year from "The Call of Duty" by Thomas S. Monson

> *"What does it mean to magnify a calling? It means to build it up in dignity and importance, to make it honorable and commendable in the eyes of all men, to enlarge and strengthen it, to let the light of heaven shine through it to the view of other men. And how does one magnify a calling? Simply by performing the service that pertains to it."*
>
> We are called to be faithful in whatever we do. Just as a teacher is trained to educate a body of students, the teacher does not want to be mediocre. A teacher who truly has a heart for teaching and learning and a passion to work with students would want to have excellent performance in the classroom.
>
> In the United States of America, there is a platform to celebrate excellent teaching. A teacher is usually named teacher of the year at a local school. That teacher then goes on to compete for the District Teacher of the Year. The selected District Teacher of the Year goes on to compete for the State Teacher of the Year. Once reaching the pinnacle of excellence by being chosen the State Teacher of the Year, she now becomes qualified to compete for National Teacher of the Year. This is how you magnify a calling.
>
> In the words of Thomas S. Monson, to magnify a calling "means to build it up in dignity and importance, to make it honorable and commendable in the eyes of all men." Therefore, whatever our chosen professions may be, let us do our very best to shine.

The message here is for us to be diligence in all that we say and in all that do.

1987 Quote of the Year from "Keeping Life's Demands in Balance" by M. Russell Ballard

"Sometimes we need a personal crisis to reinforce in our minds what we really value and cherish. The scriptures are filled with examples of people facing crises before learning how to better serve God and others. Perhaps if you too, search your hearts and courageously assess the priorities in your life, you may discover, as I did that you need a better balance among your priorities. All of us must come to an honest, open self-examination, an awareness within as to who and what we want to be."

Challenges keep us going and growing. Therefore, we will sometimes face challenges and obstacles, "wherefore ye must press forward with a steadfastness in Christ, having a perfect brightness of hope and a love of God and of all men, wherefore, if ye shall press forward, feasting upon the words of Christ and endure to the end, behold, thus saith the Father: ye shall have eternal life."

It is important that we understand that there must be an opposition in all things. If one does not experience sadness, he or she will not be able to appreciate the good time.

The message for us here is to understand that we are strengthen through our adversities.

1988 Quote of the Year from "Happiness through Service" by Thomas S. Monson

> *"In all of your incomings and outgoings, may you have peace in your hearts, may you have tranquility in your homes, and may you have the Spirit of the Lord Jesus Christ in your souls."*
>
> In everything we do in life, we need to keep in our minds and in our hearts the light of our Savior Jesus Christ, because through him, all things are possible. If we fail to maintain this pattern of thought, we will eventually succumb to the challenges of this world. According to scriptures, we are reminded to be of good cheer because Christ has overcome the world.
>
> By Christ overcoming the world, we too have the potential to overcome the world and temptations that the adversary brings forth. We must have faith in the Savior and act on it, seeking good and becoming more like Jesus Christ and sharing the light of Christ. We do this so that we too may overcome the world.

The message here is for us to understand if we are obedient to God's will, He will give us a peace of mind that passes all understanding.

1989 Quote of the Year from "Alternate Voices" by Dallin H. Oaks

> *"Some of life's most complicated decisions involve mixtures of good and evil. To what extent can one seek the benefit of something good one desires when this can only be done by simultaneously promoting something bad one opposes? That is a personal decision, but it needs to be made with a sophisticated view of the entire circumstance with a prayer for heavenly guidance."*
>
> Our personal decisions must be carefully considered because even the smallest decisions can have a big impact that we cannot always see the consequences now. Our Father in Heaven see's our potential and who he wants us to become, it is important to have daily prayer and ask for guidance on how we can better ourselves. By seeking the Lord's counsel through prayer and scripture study we are blessed and receive Heaven's help.
>
> Should we fail to seek spiritual guidance, we are more vulnerable to the adversary and his evil ways. But as we have hope and do God's will, we are able to escape the adversary's ways and feel God's hand in our lives.

The message here is that we all have free agency to choose as we please; thus we must understand that our personal decision must be made carefully.

1990 Quote of the Year from "Home First" by Rex D. Pinegar

"Within that 'wonderful chaos' of our family all is obviously not perfect. There are problems in our family, as in many families—challenges related to serious illness, aging parents, schooling, employment, and others. However, individual burdens and concerns may be lightened by the power of a family united in mutual love and support and in prayers of faith."

Our families are the most important social unit and ordained of God. It is vital that we strive to do all we can to maintain a spirit of love and peace in all of our relationships and in our homes. In doing this, we will find that our love for our family members will grow and the Spirit of God will have a greater influence upon us. According to Galatians 5:23, the fruits of the spirit are love, joy, and peace. We feel these gentle feelings as we love one another.

If we do not do our best to maintain our relationships with one another and love each other, we again fall into the arms and temptations of the adversary and he works hard to tear apart families because he understands how important they are. But as we do simple things to uplift each other and serve, we feel the importance of families in a personal way and we strengthen our testimonies of the Gospel of Jesus Christ.

The message here is for us to cherish our families for as long as we live on this Earth.

1991 Quote of the Year from "Called to Serve" by L. Tom Perry

> *"The discipline contained in daily obedience and clean living and wholesome lives builds an armor around you of protection and safety from the temptations that beset you as you proceed through mortality."*
>
> Obedience is important when we seek to become more like our Savior Jesus Christ. It really is the small and simple things that we must do in order to put our armor on. Having a relationship with Heavenly Father and keeping his commandments are important. When we may go astray and find ourselves off of the straight and narrow path, we must recognize it and do our best to get back on the right path and put on the armor of God. The armor of God are simple things such as prayer, scripture study and Church attendance.
>
> If we do fall into the temptations of the Devil and stay on his path for longer periods of time we will find ourselves not so happy, easily falling into temptation and not feel the spirit as much in our lives. We will also see ourselves easily aggravated and upset at things that we should not be upset about. Therefore it is so important to keep God in our heart AT ALL TIMES and always strive to do God's will and be obedient to his commandments and acknowledge his son Jesus Christ.

The message here is for us to always stay in obedience to God's word at all times.

1992 Quote of the Year from "Be Men" by Carlos E. Asay

> *"It seems that everyone at some time or another is invited by peers to smoke, drink, steal, or engage in other immoral acts, all under the pretense of manhood. And when someone refuse to participate, he is often ridiculed and called names like pansy, mamma's boy, idiot, chicken, sissy, and religious fanatic. Such names are used by peers who equate manliness with the ability to drink liquor, blow tobacco smoke out of all the facial cavities, sow one's wild oats like some animal on the street, and break moral laws without a twinge of conscience."*

The world's view of fun and happiness is polar opposite from the view of our Heavenly Father's perspective of what true and lasting happiness is. Oft times we are bombarded by sin and temptations and in many instances sin is seen as the only way to be happy. The adversary wants us to believe that sin is somehow the way to happiness, however as we learned from studies this is not the case "wickedness never was happiness." If we are seeking true and lasting happiness, the only way to obtain it is through the gospel of Jesus Christ.

Daily communication with God is key, along with scripture study and a higher moral standard of living. In doing this we will gain our Heavenly Father's approval and the outside voices and ridicule we receive from the world will eventually be silenced. We cannot give into the pressure to transgress God's laws, it will only bring shame and sadness, contrary to God's glorious plan for us.

The lesson here for us is that we must stay focus on the word of God and do not allow ourselves to be tricked by the adversary.

1993 Quote of the Year from "The Principle of Work" F. David Stanley

"We are what we are as a people because our ancestors were not afraid of honest, hard work. Our forefathers understood the necessity of it; sheer survival demanded it. A common ingredient among all successful people is an understanding of what constitutes paying the price of success. Basic in that formula of paying the price is an inner gift of determination that 'I'll do whatever it takes." That means, 'I'll work hard, with integrity, to achieve my goal." Hard work is a blessing of God. It involves going after it 'with all your heart, might, mind and strength.' That alone is the difference between the average and the excellent."

We as children of our Heavenly Father want to become something great. It is a natural desire inside of us that wants to succeed and be happy with our lives. In order for us to find true happiness, we must first accept the fact that we are under God's will and look for ways to improve ourselves. If we work hard spiritually and do our VERY best we are promised that the Lord will make up the difference. We must also be patient in our doings and understand that the Lord's timing is perfect.

A very good quote given by Thomas S. Monson that I think goes along very well with this concept is "may we choose the harder right, instead of the easier wrong." God has given us our agency, or the ability to choose for ourselves. As we seek to make the correct choices in life, whether it be for work, marriage or temporal situations the counsel given from Monson will help us make the correct and more important decision.

The message here is that if we work hard, it will eventually pay off.

1994 Quote of the Year from "Walk with Me" by Elaine L. Jack

"Indeed, the path is not soft, green grass; it is not without hardship and heartache. It is often an uphill climb strewn with rocks, many of them in the shape of mighty boulders. We can't predict what our challenges will be because our lives are all different. Though the path is narrow, our moves are not scripted. There are diversions which attempt to lure us from the straight and narrow. It is our covenants that are the road signs to eternal life. Just as it is more difficult to read the signs on the main road from a side street, so too it is more difficult to hear the still, small voice of warnings, rough road ahead, when we have distanced ourselves from our covenants."

We do not just smoothly sail through life. Our experience on this Earth is truly tested. James Cleveland has said it best: "Nobody told me that the road was going to be easy." He is right. The road can sometimes be very difficult. We, nonetheless, possess the power within to withstand.

My mother always used to tell me that "trouble don't always last." With this lesson, I was always able to patiently face challenges. I had that hope my mother instilled in me that the trouble won't always be there. Her insightful wisdom helped me through many rough days. Thanks God for her encouragement along the way and along those lines.

We must seek the pathway to Heaven, regardless of the stumbling blocks in the road. We have to find ways to succeed in our spiritual endeavors that line up with the scriptures.

The message for us is to have confidence in the small voices that speaks within us and obey the spirit as it directs our path.

1995 Quote of the Year from "We Have a Work to Do" by Gordon B. Hinckley

> *"My beloved associates, far more of us need to awake and arouse our faculties to an awareness of the great everlasting truths of the gospel of Jesus Christ. Each of us can do a little better than we have been doing. We can be a little more kind. We can be a little more merciful. We can be a little more forgiving. We can put behind us our weaknesses of the past, and go forth with new energy and increased resolution to improve the world about us, in our homes, in our places of employment, in our social activities. We have work to do, you and I, so very much of it. Let us roll up our sleeves and get at it, with a new commitment."*

It is good to hear the encouraging words that we can do better. Most of the times we hear criticism after criticism. It is understood here that we should strive to do better and be better in our communication skills with one another. I like the encouragement that points out that we can be a little more kind. Sometimes, we are a bit mean and rude without actually meaning it. However, if we get in the practice of just being naturally kind, we would not have that problem to worry about.

The call for us to be a little bit more merciful can be answered if we give yielding ears to this effort. Sometimes, as humans, we are unnecessarily tough and mean to people for no reason. So, sure, we care be a bit kinder. We need to soften our speech, our tone and our reactions in responding to challenging times.

We have so much work to get done. Therefore, it is pertinent that we remain focus and begin to navigate in a direction that promises success.

The message here for us is that we need to improve ourselves so that we better serve humanities.

1996 Quote of the Year from "Finding Joy in Life" by Richard G. Scott

> *"We have so much freedom, so many opportunities to develop our unique personalities and talents, our individual memories, and our personalized contributions. Truly life is beautiful. Do you take time to discover each day how beautiful your life can be? How long has it been since you watched the sun set? The departing rays kissing the clouds, trees, hills and lowlands good night, sometimes tranquilly, sometimes with exuberant bursts of color and form."*

As with all children, if they are given too much freedom, they might cross the line and enter into unwelcoming territories. We must certainly avoid that snare in the road. We sometimes don't express the appreciation for the many great opportunities that life offers us. We have a collection of talents, sweet memories and contributions that makes life truly exciting.

In the midst of the hustle and bustle, we need to take time out to observe nature or the creation and express appreciation for all things made. We need the tranquil moment to magnify by capturing the beauty of this world and offering praises to the Savior for the aesthetic gift called the Earth.

Take time for yourselves and be vigilant in observing nature knowing that God has put everything on the Earth for our good. We ought to never stop giving the praises to God for His blessings upon our lives. We are to always remain grateful and appreciative.

The message for us here is to take time to live and enjoy the Earth one day at a time.

1997 Quote of the Year from "As Good As Our Bond" by Sheldon F. Child

> *"Honesty and integrity are not old-fashioned principles.*
> *They are just as viable in today's world. We have been*
> *taught that when we say we will do something, we do it;*
> *when we make a commitment, we honor it; when we are*
> *given a calling, we fulfill it. When we borrow something,*
> *we return it; when we have a financial obligation, we pay*
> *it and when we enter into an agreement, we keep it."*

Do we live our lives by principles or do we just live from day to day without any regards to our purpose for being on the earth? We must strive to become men and women who keep and honor the commitment we make. We are always to be truthful and not deceitful to our fellow mankind.

In dealing with people, we must strive to practice honesty and integrity. We must know when to say yes and we must know when to say no to certain request. There will be times, when we are not in a position to do something. Rather than standing a person up, we must communicate directly with the individual always expressing honest deed. When we do this, we will become more respected in society. We must learn to fulfill every obligation we make.

We owe it to ourselves and to our fellow-citizens to be people of integrity and honesty. There are so many modes in which we can use to communicate with one another from across the globe. There is no excuse to set the records straight. We must be respectful in communicating with one another.

The message for us here is to be a man or woman of our words and never let anyone discover us being anything other than honest.

1998 Quote of the Year from "Put Your Shoulder to the Wheel" by Neal A. Maxwell

> *"When the time comes, young men, make your career choices. Know that whether one is a neurosurgeon, forest ranger, mechanic, farmer, or teacher is a matter of preference not of principle. While those career choices are clearly very important, these do not mark your real career path. Instead, brethren, you are sojourning sons of God who have been invited to take the path that leads home. There, morticians will find theirs is not the only occupations to become obsolete. But the capacity to work and work wisely will never become obsolete.*
> *And neither will the ability to learn. Meanwhile, my young brethren, I have not seen any perspiration-free shortcuts to the celestial kingdom; there is no easy escalator to take us there."*

We must strive for excellence in whatever we do. We should prayerfully consider our choices as we pursue a career. Remember, it is not the career or job that makes the man. It is the man that makes the job. We must forever be mindful that as we seek God's advice and direction for our career choices, we would be blessed in our chosen fields.

I like how Neal A. Maxwell puts it: "we are sojourning sons of God." We are only on this Earth for a short while. Therefore, we must seek the Master's will for our lives. If we do what he leads us to do, we can never go wrong. Therefore, it is so important that we follow the guidance of the Holy Spirit.

Our ultimate goal is to reach Heaven and, I believe, that Maxwell puts it best: there is no easy escalator to get us there.

The message for us here is to make our plans in alignment with God's will and we will be successful in making it to our heavenly destination.

1999 Quote of the Year from "This is Our Day" by James E. Faust

> *"We should seize every opportunity to move forward in faith, looking beyond the year 2000 into a future bright with hope, acknowledging that all good gifts come by divine providence. With such increased knowledge comes a higher responsibility. If we work hard, wisely manage our personal stewardships, and live providently, the Lord will prosper us in our use of the heightened knowledge to advance holy work."*

This is a call and challenge for us to take full advantage of the many splendid blessings that our Creator has in store for us. We are encouraged to look ahead into the 21st Century with faith and hope knowing that everything is already predestined by God.

We must always be aware of the fact that to whom much is given much is also required. In understanding that all gifts comes by divine providence, we should always be responsible enough to seek knowledge of all good things. In whatever we do or whatever path we choose, we must wisely and patiently wait on the Lord to do His job.

The message here is for us to seek His path for our lives in order to advance ourselves towards heightened knowledge.

2000 Quote of the Year from "Future Leaders" Harold G. Hilliam

> *"I urge you young people to develop the habit of always showing respect, courtesy, and deference to your parents and others, especially those who are older than you. My father taught me that every person in and out of the church has a title, such as Mr., Mrs., Brother, Sister, Bishop, Elder, or President, and that they should be addressed with respect. When I was six years old, my father taught me with firmness that I had shown a lack of respect by being so casual to an older person. I have never forgotten that experience, nor have I after 60 years forgotten the name of the grocer. I even remember his first name."*

Developing a culture of respect for the elders is an important gesture. My mother always taught me to respect my elders. In South Carolina, we grew up with addressing every one with an appropriate title. We never called an older person by his or her first name. That was a no-no.

It may seem like a small matter to some. Yet, acknowledging people in an appropriate manner is the right thing to do. To do otherwise would be a demonstration of the lack of respect. By addressing people with appropriate titles, we naturally and immediately gain respect from the recipients each and every time we demonstrate respect ourselves.

We must pride ourselves in being respectful and showing to others that we are kind and caring human beings.

Byron S. Brown

The message for us here is simply to be respectful to the elderly at all times no matter whom the person might be or what title the person might hold in society.

2001 Quote of the Year from "Focus and Priorities" by Dallin H. Oaks

> *"Because of increased life expectancies and modern timesaving devices, most of us have far more discretionary time than our predecessors. We are accountable for how we use that time. The significance of our increased discretionary time has been magnified many times by modern data-retrieval technology. For good or for evil, devices like the internet ant the compact disc have put at our fingertips an incredible inventory of information, insights, and images. With greatly increased free time and vastly more alternatives for its use, it is prudent to review the fundamental principles that should guide us. Temporal circumstances change, but the eternal laws and principles that should guide our choices never change."*

Time is of the essence. We all know when we were born. None of us, however, knows exactly when we are going to die. We must therefore be held accountable our time on this Earth. As stated earlier, on my grandmother's 100th birthday, I asked her what she thought contributed to her long life. She sharply and immediately responded with confidence and vigor: "Just do the right thing and mine your own business."

In just one complete sentence, my grandmother was astutely aware of her time on earth. She was pleased with her life. She had always asked the Lord to allow her to reach 100 years of life. She was able to reach that milestone without any problems. The grace of God was upon her life.

It should be our goal to live as long as we can and as healthy as we can being led by a spirit of love and cooperation with all mankind.

The message for us here to realize is that tomorrow is not promised to anyone.

2002 Quote of the Year from "The Road We Call Life" Life by Ben B. Banks

> *"The patterns you establish in your youth may accompany you throughout the rest of your mortal life. By making the right choices now, you will be able to take the path that will help you endure the coldest and bleakest moments later. Yes, life's journeys can have many ups and downs. Yes, there will be days when you will feel the going is tough. But as you stay on the right path, the reward at the end of life's journey is well worth the moments of adversity you experience along the way."*

We need to watch our lives on a daily basis because we begin to set patterns at a young age. The habits we establish as children will follow us into our adult life. At a very young age, children often face peer pressures and are often led into conflicting spiritual and social activities. These activities have the potential to ruin a person's character early on. This is why it is important for parents to intervene with prayer and biblical studies into the lives of their children.

The bible points out that parents ought to train their children in the ways of the Lord and when they grow up, they will not depart from the truth. This is more like a guaranteed promissory note.

If parents want their children to succeed, it becomes necessary for them to contribute into their children's lives. There is a popular saying that supports this thought: "If there is no deposit, there will be no returns. This is a powerful statement that should not go unnoticed.

The message here for us is to assist our children early on by teaching them how to sow good seeds in hope of reaping many blessings in their lives for many years to come.

2003 Quote of the Year from "Words to Live" by James M. Dunn

> *"Successfully working our way through life, while keeping our eye on life's true purposes, blesses us both here and hereafter. So our earthly mission hasn't much to do at all with our mortal careers. It has, however, everything to do with preparing for our immortal destiny."*

This life is a spiritual journey. When I was a child, one of my favorite songs claims these words: "This world is not my home. I am just here for a little while. I am just passing through." That is exactly what we are doing, just passing through. Actually, life is nothing but a fleeting moment. We must enjoy it and do the right thing while we are here.

In life, we must make sacrifices in order to be able to be a positive influence to our contemporaries. We must stay on course with the path that God has planned for us. How do we recognize that plan? We do so by staying constantly in prayers and in reading God's words and remaining vigilant in dealing with people from all walks of life.

We must seek for positive solutions in our lives that would put us on a path to eternal life with the Father.

The message here is for us to not rely on our own thinking but to acknowledge God in all our ways.

2004 Quote of the Year from "The Finished Story" by Gayle M. Clegg

> *"We have to keep writing, keep walking, keep serving and accepting new challenges to the end of our own story. We each must find and finish our own story, but how much sweeter the telling when encouragement is called out, when arriving at our destination is valued and celebrated, however long ago the journey commenced."*

Everyone has a story to tell. What is your story? Our stories can perhaps help shape people in a positive manner if shared. You have experienced something that can help someone to achieve and accomplish a goal. Your story has the power to transform lives. When others learn of what you have experienced it can strengthen their hope.

We ought not to be shy about sharing how we dealt with adversities in our lives and overcame our own fears. With our victorious stories, others are able to gain courage. All we have to do is share our stories with them with enthusiasm and conviction. They will begin to listen to us and trust our judgement.

People are made to feel special when they are freely able to communicate with one another.

The message here is to know that you are not the only one who experienced hardship in your life and to realize that you are more than a conqueror.

2005 Quote of the Year from "The Virtue of Kindness" by Joseph B. Wirthlin

> *"Kindness is the essence of greatness and the fundamental characteristic of the noblest men and women I have known. Kindness is a passport that opens doors and fashions friends. It softens hearts and molds relationships that can last lifetimes. Kind words not only lift our spirits in the moment they are given, but they can linger with us over the years. Kindness should permeate all of our words and actions."*
>
> We must come to the realization that kindness is a great attribute to exhibit. When we are kind one to another, it helps us become a united society. A kind thought, a kind word, a kind deed are all deeply appreciated when others are aware of our well doing.
>
> Kindness is a friendly disposition. The bible says that if a man wants to have friends, he must first show himself to be friendly. No one wants to be around people who are always bitter, grouchy, complaining. Human beings have the tendency to resonate with that which is pleasant.
>
> We know that misery loves company. Therefore, we ought to remove ourselves from negative people. We should greet each brand new day with a spirit of cheerfulness and admiration for life without hesitation. Be a positive force and not a negative weight to the world.

The message here is for us to understand we can gain more friendship with honey than with vinegar.

2006 Quote of the Year from "Our rising Generation" by Ronald A. Rasband

> *"In these perilous times, as youth are faced with this increased adversity, we can learn from others. In the armed forces, particularly in all the navies throughout the world, every seaman understands one phrase that is a clarion call for immediate help, no matter what he is doing or where he is on the ship. The call is 'All hands on deck.' Many a battle at sea has been worn or lost by the response to this call. We all need to respond to the call for 'all hands on deck' as it pertains to our youth and young single adults. We must all look for opportunities to bless the youth whether or not we are currently closely associated."*

The bible says that perilous times shall come. For fifty years, I experienced a number of perilous situations. However, I trusted in a being higher than myself. In fact, I trusted in the almighty God who brought me out of many unpredictable circumstances. Adversity continues to rise one after the other. Rather than allowing a particular situation to get you down, you need to commit the situation into the hands of the Lord.

Adversity comes to strengthen you. It has been stated time and time again that the unexamined life is not worth living. Our lives are filled with test and challenges. We must learn to take every experience, every setback and every challenge as learning opportunities. Such opportunities will lead us to a peace of mind that passes all understanding.

There must be an all hands on deck experience in helping our youth to escape danger in the midst of life's battles.

The message for us here is to teach the youth how to contend with adversity no matter how stiff the challenge may be.

2007 Quote of the Year from "Gratitude a Path to Happiness" by Bonnie D. Parkin

> *"The kind of gratitude that receives even tribulations with thanksgiving requires a broken heart and a contrite spirit, humility to accept that which we cannot change, willingness to turn everything over to the Lord—even when we do not understand, thankfulness for hidden opportunities yet to be revealed. Then comes a sense of peace. Adversity compels us to go to our knees; does gratitude for adversity do that as well?"*

As Christians, we must be able to demonstrate humility. We must not allow our self-will to get the best of us. We must remain grateful to God for every experience we encounter on a daily basis. Whether the experience is positive or negative, it comes to teach us a very much needed lesson in life.

Actually, in life, it always seems that we have two choices facing us. One choice is that we humble ourselves unto what the Father asks of us or we can regrettably allow God Himself to humble us. It is far better that we yield to a spirit of humility.

We must train ourselves and our children how to walk in obedience to His divine purpose for our lives. We should not wait for adversity to come our way before recognizing the supreme power of God.

The message here is that we will humble ourselves daily that we might learn how to walk in the spirit.

2008 Quote of the Year from "One among the Crowd" by Dennis B. Neuenschwander

> *"Struggling through the crowds of the world can be lonely and hard. Their pull and tug on the individual who wishes to step away to something better can be very strong and very difficult to overcome."*
>
> As we strive to advance in society, remember that there will be people who will try to get in your way. All you have to do is stay on course with your vision to excel. People will be jealous of your effort. Pay that no attention. Continue to always embrace the ideal of hard work and commitment. These may be the defining moments of our lives. No one can live your dream for you. Therefore, don't let anyone stand in your way of progression. Let no one stand in the way of your vision. Let no one tell you that you cannot do something. Stick with a determined mind, heart and soul with the vision or goal that you have set for yourself.
>
> No one ever achieved anything great by giving up. Perseverance and endurance are what we need in order to obtain victory in the end.
>
> When we have fierce determination, bold courage and uncommon strength to push ahead, our drive to succeed makes it easier to achieve the goals we set for ourselves.

The message here for us to understand is not to let anything deter us from marching forward and onward.

2009 Quote of the Year from "Unselfish Service" by Dallin H. Oaks

"We live in a time when sacrifice is definitely out of fashion, when the outside forces that taught our ancestors the need for unselfish cooperative service have diminished. Someone has called this the 'me' generation—a selfish time when everyone seems to be asking, what's in it for me? Even some who should know better seem to be straining to win the praise of those who mock and scoff."

God is looking for committed people who are willing to serve without procrastination. Many times we put off what we can do today for tomorrow. Sometimes we look for the easy way out. Other times, we are not as sharp, focus and alert as we ought to be. Selfless living is what God's is expecting of us. We need to become more cognizant of this fact.

Our ancestors worked tirelessly in carving a path for us to succeed in life. Yet, sometimes, it appears that we easily forget the pain and anguish they experienced in making sacrifice. They marched, died and bleed for us to behold a better world than what they witnessed. We must grow to appreciate this kind of remarkable strength.

Our ancestors endured turbulent times without excuses, without complaints, and without fear. They were unafraid to protest on behalf of our future. Therefore, we too must learn how to sacrifice. We must roll our sleeps up, charge our batteries up, and press forward in the midst of adversities in sacrificing ourselves for the better cause of humanity.

The message here for us is that we have learned how to make sacrifices as our ancestors did in order to make the world a better place to live.

2010 Quote of the Year from "Remember Who You Are!" By Elain S. Dalton

> *"The world would have you believe that you are not significant—that you are out of fashion and out of touch. The world calls to you with unrelenting, noisy voices to 'live it up,' 'try everything,' 'experiment and be happy.' You must have the courage to stand out to."*

There is no doubt that you are important. Don't listen to the voice of the adversary. You know your strength. You know your limitation. You know yourself. Each of us is significant to the body of Christ. We all play different roles in the body of Christ.

Don't let anyone else determine your destiny. I cannot stress enough that God made us the head and not the tail. On this note, we must understand that He has it in his divine plan for us to live superb lives. We are His children. Therefore, we have special privileges on Earth.

The world tries to tempt us by offering many challenges to our existence. By uttering, 'live it up,' 'try everything,' 'experiment and be happy.' We do not have to listen to this sort of nonsense. This is only noise that the world screams. Disregard the noise of evil.

The message for us here is to be a new and different person in everything we say and do.

2011 Quote of the Year from "Opportunities to Do Good" by Henry B. Eyring

> *"All people are happier and feel more self-respect when they can provide for themselves and their family and then reach out to take care of others. I have been grateful for those who helped me meet my needs. I have been even more grateful over the years for those who helped me become self-reliant. And then I have been most grateful for those who showed me how to use some off my surplus to help others."*

Self-Reliance is a great concept. We must learn how to plan financially for ourselves and our family. When we are able to afford the necessities for ourselves and our family, we truly become livelier and happier people. No family needs to experience the stress of financial burdens.

Bringing children into the world without strategic financial planning is a tremendous disadvantage to the children. This forces much burden to enter into the home, thus causing more severe problems. Proper preparation is needed in order to prevent financial hardship on the family.

I love the two great pieces of sound advice that many great people refer to in strategizing for financial success. One proverb says, "Give a man a fish, he will eat for a day. Teach a man how to fish, he will eat for a lifetime." This makes pretty good sense to me. The other piece of wisdom lies within these words: "Give a man a dollar, he will have money for a day. Teach a man how to work, he will have money for a lifetime." I call this simple wisdom.

The message here for us is to "teach," and in doing so we will be able to "reach" others.

2012 Quote of the Year from "Sacrifice" by Dallin H. Oaks

"Our lives of service and sacrifice are the most appropriate expressions of our commitment to serve the Master and our fellowmen."

I am big on the ideas of service. The great philosopher, Horace Mann, offers this challenge: "Be ashamed to die until you have won some victory for humanity." We should not be selfish. We should not sit around and do for ourselves and disregard the rest of the word. We must be willing to make some sacrifices in order to help others. Helping can be as simple as encouraging someone to do something positive.

Serving others is a kind and gracious deed. You have the power to encourage others to do well. Extending a helping hand to others adds blessings into your life. When you serve humanity, you serve God.

For the past seven years, I have organized and promoted the South Carolina Heritage and Humanities Festival. In this event, people are able to express their gifts and talents. Cultures come together that otherwise do not generally assemble together. People feel strengthened and encouraged by the influx of diversity in age, race and religious beliefs.

The message for us here is to be willing to help others with the gifts and talents that God has given each of us.

2013 Quote of the Year from "The Home: The School of Life" by Erique R. Falabella

> *"The words 'I love you,' 'thank you,' and 'forgive me' are like balm for the soul. They transform tears into happiness. They provide comfort to the weighed-down soul, and they confirm the tender feelings of our heart. Just as plants withers with the lack of precious water, our love languishes and dies as we put to rest the words and acts of love."*
>
> When I was growing up in the late 1960's and early 1970's and listening to the radio from time to time, there was a popular phrase that I heard several times throughout the week. That thought came in these transforming words: "Love is a many splendid thing." Love, indeed, is powerful and has the potential to transform lives.
>
> It is sweet to hear the kind confession: "I love you." Words can sometimes be healing. Just to hear someone say, "I love you," and especially when they mean it, is within itself transforming. Love is a many splendid thing. Love is an action verb that is used when someone wants to connect with another individual. There are several types of love. Nonetheless, when one demonstrates the love of God, he gains the power to transform negativity into positive experiences.
>
> We cannot love unless we forgive our brothers and sisters of their transgression. "To err is human. But to forgive is divine." Let us forgive one another of their wrongdoing, so that healing might immediately take root in all of our hearts.

The message for us here is to love, forgive and express appreciation to each other.

2014 Quote of the Year from "Let's Not Take the Wrong Way" by Claudio D. Zivic

> *"There are some mistakes that may be serious,*
> *and if we do not correct them in time, they can*
> *permanently lead us off the right path. If we repent*
> *and accept correction, these experiences will allow*
> *us to humble ourselves and change our actions."*

During my fifty years of peril, I have obviously made hundreds of mistakes. None of us is perfect. Yet, we strive daily for perfection. The good thing about serving a loving and forgiving God is that He looks beyond our faults and sees our needs. That is a tremendous blessing.

When our children make mistakes, we must be willing to accept that fact that they made a mistake and correct them at that time. It is not acceptable to cover up their mistakes, it would only lead to further detriment in the future for the children.

When we make mistakes as adults, or our young ones make mistakes, it is best that we correct the problem immediately. As we acknowledge our faults, we humble ourselves. When we are humble, we can learn and begin to grow from the experience. If we make spiritual mistakes, all we need to do is repent and ask the loving Heavenly Father to forgive us of our transgressions.

The message here for us to understand is that all humans have sinned and fell short of the glory of God realizing that there is nothing to be ashamed of as we strive to please the Father.

2015 Quote of the Year from "Choose to Believe" by L. Whitney Clayton

> *"All of us will, at some time or another, have to traverse our own spiritual wilderness and undertake our own rugged emotional journeys. In those moments, however dark or seemingly hopeless they may be, if we search for it, there will always be a spiritual light that beckons to us, giving us the hope off rescue and relief."*

Every man must bear his own burden. We are constantly being challenged in order to move to the next level in life. There is no such thing as a "battle-free," life. We all grow from challenges. Through adversities, we get to know our own strengths and weaknesses. It does not feel good to be challenged. However, the victory tastes sweet after we have gone through tribulations.

Since the battle-free life does not really exist, we must learn to stand firmly on the foundation of truth. We must always remember that Jesus Christ himself faced adversities. His triumphant strategies was always to remember that it was the Heavenly Father inspired him to do what he was doing at that particular time. Staying obedient plays a significant role, as we continue to forge ahead knowing that our resolves will continue to be challenged.

What we experience with others during conflicting times is truly an emotional journey. Whitney Clayton offers us best hope: "In those moments, however dark or seemingly hopeless they may be, if we search for it, there will always be a spiritual light that beckons to us, giving us the hope."

The message for us here is know that we will be tested and we will have trials but there is no reason to give up hope.

2016 Quote of the Year from "To The Rescue: We Can Do It" by Mervyn Arnold

"No matter our age, we are all called to go to the rescue."

We are never too young to help out in a crisis. We are never too old to heroically respond to a crisis. We are never too young or old to serve. We are called to serve. We should be elated of the opportunity to rescue someone from a perplexing situation. Love encourages us to bail people out when they are in deep trouble.

We can rescue others through prayer. The bible teaches us that men are always to pray. When was the last time you prayed for someone in need of a miracle? Remember, prayer changes things. We possess rescuing power through the sincere lyric of prayer. In our daily lives, prayer is our weapon through all sorts of adversities.

We are able to demonstrate the love of God in our efforts to rescue family members or friends. We continually gain power through the words of our sacred prayers.

The message here is that we ought to love one another enough to be willing to launch out into the deep to rescue a friend or a stranger.

2017 Quote of the Year from "Stand Up Inside and Be all In" by Gary B. Sabin

> *"May we recalculate our route if need be and look forward with great hope and faith. May we stand up inside by being valiant and all in."*

This is a call for full surrender. When it comes down to our lives, we must be able to put 100% effort in the chasing our dreams. We must commit 100% to praying, fasting, reading and studying the word of God. No one does exceptionally well by putting in minimum effort.

In the journey of life, we are urged to make a complete surrender to the Master. When we are all in, we are able to see the whole view. Seeing matters partially does not provide the advantage of seeing matters fully. We cannot calculate correctly only having access to partial viewing.

We must recalculate our routes, if we are not fully participating in whatever endeavor we seek or employ. Our whole mind, body, soul and spirit must be into it. No matter what that "it" is, give your full and undivided attention to it. It is a call for total commitment.

The message here for us is to stand up and be counted.

Chapter 15

A Plea to Avoid Drinking and Driving

Dear Friends:

No one knows the pain more than I do in losing a love one in a Driving Under the Influence situations. My father's life ended all too soon on September 23, 19967. Fifty years later, I still wonder about the good life I could possibly have had with my dad. Someone else took that privilege away from me, a privilege that will never be recognized. Therefore, here I wish to present an argument to get as many of you to campaign against drinking and driving. Drinking and driving is a dangerous act and can bring about serious problems leading up to death. Not for one second would I want anyone to experience the devastating loss of a love one. Here is the good news about drunk driving facts. Drunk driving is a 100% preventable choice. No one forces a person to engage in drinking and then forces the person to become the designated driver. If something is avoidable, then it only makes sense not to cause greater harm upon yourselves, your family members or anyone whom you may come in contact or impact with as you drive.

According to Mothers Against Drinking and Driving, two out of three people will be impacted by drunk driving in their lifetime. The problem with this is that you never know who the two of three people may consist of in the years to come. Sadly, those people could be a father, brother, uncle, nephew or cousin and friend.

Although 0.8% blood alcohol level is the illegal limit in all fifty states, we should participate in discouraging anyone from driving whom we may have knowledge of that might consume alcohol regularly. With this knowledge, I ask of everyone who reads this book to in your own small ways to fight against drunk driving. Drunk driving too often ends up costing someone's life. Compiling with the case of death is also the denying of love ones to ever again communicate with the deceased victims. This causes a huge void in a person's life. As you navigate throughout society, I encourage you to speak out against drunk driving. Drunk driving is an unfair advantage to victims. While all drunk driving accidents do not end up in a fatality, it is of paramount importance that we discourage even the idea of drinking and driving period.

Drunk driving is a major offense and it should be condemned at all times at all cost. As we all have become accustomed to the idea that friends don't let friends drink and drive, we must also become accustomed to the reality that we must stand up and speak out against drunk driving.

Reach out and help someone out by fighting strongly against drunk driving and drinking. If someone was not drinking and driving, my father Samuel George Brown would not have been killed.

Go and speak out against drinking and driving. This is all what the S.O.A.K. (Speaking Out Against Known cases of Drinking and Driving

Campaign of South Carolina is all about on the 50th Anniversary of the death of my father, Samuel George Brown.

As a result of this 50th year commemoration, I encourage each of you to speak out and be a hero.

Dad continue to rest in peace!

Sincerely,
Byron S. Brown

About the Author

Byron Sylvester Brown was born in Eutawville, South Carolina, on April 23, 1965 the seventh child of a Brick Mason and Carpenter Samuel George Brown and a housewife, Annie Lee (Charlotte) Jackson Brown. Ms. Sarah Sumpter served as midwife to his birth. Brown's birth came at the end of the Civil Rights Movement and nearly 100 years after the end of the Civil War and the assassination of the United States 16th President, Abraham Lincoln who issued the Emancipation Proclamation. This proclamation has significance to Brown. His maternal great-great grandmother came to Charleston, South Carolina on the ship from West Africa. His grandmother, Florrie Lee Jackson who died April 29, 2012 was 100 years old. She often told him of how her great grandmother came on the ship from Africa only bringing two siblings and leaving the other 8 or 9 siblings back in Africa and that she died in 1923 at the age of 117 years old in which Jackson knew her and was 12 years old at her great-grandmother's demise. Brown's paternal great-grand parents were from the West Indies, dating back to Mr. Eddie Legree. Brown often said of himself: "I am one-third African; one-third West Indies, one-third African-American and one percent divine."

Brown's father was killed in a car accident on September 23, 1967, when he was only two years old. His mother was forced to work to raise seven children. She began working as a maid for Ms. Thelma Poag, at a Boarding House in Holly Hill, South Carolina.

In August 1971, Brown entered St. James Elementary school for the first time. He immediately began to take an interest in education. When he entered Roberts High School, he took an interest in writing, particularly. He began to serve as a contributing writer for the Holly Hill Observer. While in high school, however, he was highly discouraged by one of his teachers who told him that he was "stupid and could not learn." As a quick and thoughtless aftermath, Brown dropped out of school. His avenging angel was a next door neighbor, Mr. William James, Jr, who encouraged him and talked him into going back to school. He listened and returned to school. On June 3, 1983, Brown graduated from Holly Hill-Roberts High School, nearly at the bottom of his class due to extreme pressure and lack of confidence in teachers.

In 1983, Brown was accepted and enrolled in Morris College in Sumter, South Carolina—the same college his mother was enrolled in who had to drop out to take care of her ill father, Boston Jackson, Sr. Brown ran for vice-president of the freshman class at Morris College and won. After serving a successful year as Vice-President, he decided to run for President of the sophomore class. He won and served as President of the sophomore class. After making the honor roll a few times and becoming a Dean O.R. Ruben Scholar at Morris College. Brown's confidence in his ability was boosted. Desiring a greater academic challenge, he transferred to Norfolk State University in Norfolk, Virginia, where things were not exactly greener on the other side. Brown managed to graduate, in spite of a number of personal and financial challenges. Receiving a Bachelor of Arts degree in English was conferred to him in May 1987.

Excited about ample opportunities for success. Brown moved across the country to Los Angeles, California, hoping to become a successful writer. His cousin Theresa A. Sellers-Asbury secured living quarters for him. As a successful businesswoman working Los Angles, she encouraged Brown to seek meaningful employment. Brown worked for a few temporary agencies.

Brown later began to rent from former Hollywood Movie Star Chritopher Joy, former husband to actress Denise Williams. Brown began Christian Evangelistic work with Mr. Joy. Brown then began to publish a Christian magazine, exercising his writing skills. After a slow start with the magazine business, Brown left Lost Angeles to pursue a Master's in Public Administration at Kentucky State University in Frankfort, Kentucky.

While studying in Kentucky, Brown discovered another talent he had other than writing—public speaking. One fortunate day, Brown was able to meet William Alexander Haley, the son of Alex Haley, the author of Roots: The Saga of an American Family. Brown and Haley began to speak to students on the campus of Kentucky State University and within the community at large about the possibility of traveling to Africa as missionaries. Brown's popularity was raised and he became a more respected individual. He was then considered as the number one choice to be the keynote speaker for the upcoming black history program at the largest black church in Frankfort, Kentucky—First Corinthian Baptist Church. In February 1988, Brown took command of the stage and delivered his first-ever keynote address entitled: "African-Americans: The Pro Fighters for Equality." The standing room only church was electrified and endorsed Brown as a future leader and compared his speaking style to that of Rev. Jesse Jackson. As a result of this event, Brown as asked to be the student representative to speak at the retirement banquet of the President of Kentucky State University: Raymond M. Burse. Brown chose to read Rudyard Kipling poem, "If." Delivering this poem with poetic insight and vigor, Brown's gifts were being unfolded right before his eyes.

As Brown was graduating from Kentucky State University and had no plan sealed yet, he received a phone call from his mother stating that he had received a full scholarship to study political science at Western Michigan University. Brown accepted the Dr. Martin Luther King, Jr. Scholarship and began to work on his second Master's degree at the Kalamazoo University. He graduated in one calendar year with a Master's in political science.

Brown has literally risen from the cotton fields of South Carolina to become one of America's most unique voices as an inspiring poet, a prolific writer, a dynamic motivational speaker, an exciting educator and a compassionate human being. In the words of the Boston College scholar, Ronald Cooper points out: "A unique voice does not come along all too frequently. When one doe, it often startles the eye and ear with wonder and awe. Brown stands before an interesting crossroad in current time, a place in American history in desperate need of a strong voice, a champion of Truth. Brown does not dwell in the injustices of the past. He leaps in quantum fashion to a higher plan, the place where Truth or God exists."

Brown has been given invitations by Argeo Paul Celluci, former Governor of Massachusetts to speak at the state house in Boston. Mayor Thomas M. Menino, of the City of Boston had also invited Brown to speak at the 4th Annual African-American Achievement Award

Ceremony in 1997. In February 1999, Brown was given an invitation by the Virginia Symphony to perform at Chrysler Hall in Norfolk, Virginia reciting his original poetry in conjunction with the Symphony's music portraying people and events crucial to the American Civil Rights Movement in context of the universal quest for freedom.

In 2004, Brown received a South Carolina State Department of Education Fellowship to study at the Bread Loaf School of English at Middlebury College, where Robert Frost's poetry influences the campus in Vermont. In 2010, Brown received a National Endowment for the Humanities Fellowship to study at the University of Kansas in the Richard Wright Summer Institute—The Wright Connection, and in August 2010 Brown was elected to participate in ""We the People," Project of the National Endowment for the Humanities in the "Picturing America's Conference: Out of the South: The African American Migration, "at the Sumter County Performing Arts Center. In June 2011, Brown received a National Endowment for the Humanities Award to study Abolitionism and the Underground Railroad at Colgate University in Hamilton, New York. In June 2013, Brown received his 3rd NEH Award studying Abolitionism from the American Revolution to the Civil War: Fighting Slavery and Racial Injustice at the Library Company of Philadelphia, Pennsylvania.

Brown has served as a Cooperating English Teacher for students from Harvard University, Boston College and Boston University through the Boston Public Schools when he taught English at the Jeremiah E. Burke High School in Dorchester, Massachusetts from 1994 to 1996.

On April 1, 2009, Brown was named a United States-Russia Language, Technology Math and Science Exchange Teacher by the U.S. Department of State's Bureau of Educational and Cultural Affairs Finalist and Exchange Mentor Teacher. For the next two years, Brown officially served as a mentor for two exchange teachers from Egypt at Scott's Branch High School in Summerton, South Carolina through Clarendon School District One. This was all made possible through the American Councils for International Education in Washington, D.C.

Brown's poetry writing skills has received great recognition. Brown has won both a state-wide and national poetry contest. On April 25, 2009, Brown won 1st place in his Festival on the Avenue Poetry Contest through the Sumter County Cultural Arts Center, honoring Dr. Arthenia Jackson Bates Millican, a native South Carolina national poet, author and professor. In 2011, Brown received national recognition for his poem: "Dream Teacher," through the National Career Development Association.

Brown has recited his original poetry on stage with national poet Sonia Sanchez during a program honoring Mrs. Millican at Patriot Hall in Sumter.

Brown teaches English for the Prince George's County Public Schools in Bowie, Maryland. Prior to joining Prince George's County Public Schools, he taught in the Alexandria City Public Schools and the Commonwealth of Virginia Department of Education. Brown has been named Clarendon School District One Teacher of the Year both in 2004 and 2010. He also served as an Adjunct Professor of Political Science at Morris College for seven years—2005 to 2012. Brown serve as an advisory member of the Arthenia Jackson Bates Millican Literacy Foundation.

In 2009, Brown served as a volunteer English in Accra, Ghana and in the Volta Region in Agbozume, Ghana.

Brown is the author of three books: Courage to Strive in the Midst of Adversities: A Journey from Hopelessness to Success, Realizing Dreams from A-Z: Principles for Excellence, and Fifty Years of Peril: One Day of Illumination.

Brown is married to the former Joyce D. Ayanou and they have two children: Daniel Selase Brown and Hannah Esenam Victoria Brown, and they live in the Washington, DC Metropolitan area.